Danny's Desert Rats

Other Aladdin Paperbacks
by Phyllis Reynolds Naylor

Achingly Alice
The Agony of Alice
Alice in Lace
Alice in Rapture, Sort Of
Alice the Brave
Being Danny's Dog
The Bomb in the Bessledorf Bus Depot
The Face in the Bessledorf Funeral Parlor
The Fear Place
The Healing of Texas Jake
How I Came to Be a Writer
Keeping a Christmas Secret
King of the Playground
Outrageously Alice
The Treasure of Bessledorf Hill

Danny's Desert Rats

PHYLLIS REYNOLDS NAYLOR

ALADDIN PAPERBACKS

First Aladdin Paperbacks edition November 1999

Aladdin Paperbacks
An imprint of Simon & Schuster
Children's Publishing Division
1230 Avenue of the Americas
New York, NY 10020

Also available in an Atheneum Books for Young Readers hardcover edition.
The text for this book was set in Goudy Old Style.

Printed and bound in the United States of America
2 4 6 8 10 9 7 5 3 1

The Library of Congress has cataloged the hardcover edition as follows:
Naylor, Phyllis Reynolds.
Danny's Desert Rats / Phyllis Reynolds Naylor.-1st ed.
p. cm.
Summary: T.R. and Danny join their friends in forming a group called the Desert Rats, and their major mission for the summer is helping Paul keep his beloved cat despite their town house development's rule against pets.
ISBN 0-689-81776-2 (hc.)
[1. Cats-Fiction. 2. Pets-Fiction. 3. Clubs-Fiction.] I. Title.
PZ7.N24Dan   1998
[Fic]-dc21
97-28006
CIP   AC
ISBN 0-689-83133-1 (pbk.)

To Jesse and Jen Michael Farman

Contents

The Rats

If it hadn't been so hot outside, we wouldn't have thought of the egg. And if we hadn't thought of the egg, we wouldn't have met Miss Clark. And if we hadn't met *her*, we would have enjoyed the rest of the summer a lot more. But then, of course, there was Bonkers. . . .

"I bet you could fry an egg on that sidewalk," Danny said as we stood at the door of our town house, deciding whether or not to go out.

I grinned. "Want to try it?"

Danny looked at me and started to laugh. "Wait'll Mom leaves. She said she was going to the store."

Danny and I always think of something to do. We're a team, see. Ever since Dad left and we moved to this new development outside Chicago, Danny looks out for Mom and I look out for Danny.

It must be hard to be "man of the house" when you're only twelve. Aunt Mavis worries that when Danny starts junior high in a new school this fall, he'll get in with the wrong crowd. "One bad apple can spoil the barrel," she tells Mom. Aunt Mavis, of course, worries about everything. But I figure if Danny's job is to be "man of the house," my job is to look out for bad apples and keep Danny out of trouble.

In the heat of the summer, Rosemary Acres is like a desert. Most of the trees are shorter than Mom, who's five-foot-six. So if you want to stay cool, you have three choices: go down to the woods at one end of Lake Tarragon, swim in the pool, or stay indoors.

We hated it when we first moved here because everything's regulation blue-and-gray, there are only a handful of kids our age, and they have rules you wouldn't believe. But once we got to know those other kids, who felt just as stranded as we did, we started hanging out together and figured out how to get around the rules.

The one guy who still doesn't like Rosemary Acres is Paul Bremmer. He's thirteen, a year older than Danny, and I've never been sure exactly how Paul feels about me. He and his dad came from Oregon after Mrs. Bremmer died. They brought along their cat without asking first if pets were allowed, which of course they're not. Paul never forgave Miss Quinn, the resident manager, for making him give that cat away. We didn't realize just what it had meant to him until a few weeks before school was scheduled to start, but I'll get to that later.

"You guys eat the sandwiches I made for you?" Mom asked, coming downstairs in a sundress and sandals. "There's not a thing in this house but bread and baloney. I'm going to buy some *real* food. Anybody want to come?"

"Naw," said Danny. "We'll stay cool." We had the air-conditioning turned on high.

As soon as Mom drove off, we got an egg from the refrigerator. We could hear her engine fade away as she left Cajun Drive and headed for Ginger Avenue, one of the main roads in the development. We almost brought a town house over on Parsley Place, but Danny and I didn't want to tell people we lived on a street called Parsley. This whole development is named after spices.

We started outside in our bare feet. The cement was so hot we went back and put on sneakers without tying them. We finally chose the sidewalk near the bank of mailboxes at the corner because it never gets any shade there at all.

"Think we should wait around for the other kids?" I asked.

"Naw, let's just do it," said Danny.

We crouched down and Danny carefully broke the egg over the sidewalk. I thought it might pop and hiss the way bacon sizzles when it hits the skillet, but it didn't. It just spread out, with the yellow yolk in the middle, and finally turned a little white around the edge, but that was all.

"How long do you suppose it takes?" I asked.

"I don't know," said Danny.

"Want me to go get a fork so if somebody calls the newspaper to say there're these guys frying an egg on the sidewalk, a photographer could snap a picture of you eating breakfast?" I asked.

Danny looked as though he was considering it, but just then we saw this woman coming down the block to get her mail. We don't know many of our neighbors yet. There are a couple of lawyers who live next door to us, and a "sexy babe," as Danny calls her, who lives across the street. This was the sexy babe. She was wearing a pair of white shorts and a halter top.

"Man!" said Danny. "You can see every curve she's got, and more besides!"

"How can you see more curves than she's got?" I asked, but then she was standing right next to us, putting her key in her box.

"Hi," she said, bending over and pulling out a couple envelopes. I could see the outline of her bikini through her shorts. When she locked the box again, she asked, "What are you guys doing?"

"Trying to fry an egg," I told her.

She stared down at us. "You don't have a stove?" she joked.

Danny grinned sheepishly. "We just wanted to see how hot it was outside."

She studied us for a minute, and then said, "You're the boys who live across the street from me, aren't you? I've been meaning to talk to you. I'm going to be gone for a week, and I need someone to bring in my mail each day and water my plants. Would you do it for ten dollars?"

"Sure," Danny and I said together.

"Good. Come over this afternoon sometime and I'll give you the key." We watched as her hips swayed back and forth up the sidewalk.

Danny grinned. "Man, I wish I had that swing in *my* backyard!"

I was about to say, "What swing?" and then I got it. When you get to be Danny's age, I guess, you talk in code. Danny and Paul are always saying stuff I don't understand.

I figured that the woman must be sort of kooky, though. She didn't know anything about us, so how did she know we wouldn't steal her stuff or have a party in her house while she was away? I mean, if you were looking for responsible people, would you choose two guys who were trying to fry an egg on the side-walk?

Randall Hayes, certified genius, rode up right then on his bike. It's a great bike—green and silver. Randall's eleven, a year older than me, and he's always invent-ing stuff. If you've got a problem to solve, you take it to Randall. We didn't have to explain to him what we were doing.

"You're trying to fry an egg on the sidewalk," said Randall.

"Yeah, but it's not working," I told him.

"You've got to have it *hot* hot!" he said. "Wait here, T.R." And he rode off.

T.R. is me. I don't have real names, just initials. Mom says I was named for Theodore Roosevelt, but Grandma Flora says those are my dad's initials, that's how I got them. They all tell me I can choose any name I want to go with those initials when I grow up.

Randall, though, calls me T.R. half the time, and the rest of the time he makes up names to fit my initials. Like Texas Ranger. Or Trade Route. This time, when he came back, he said, "Hey, Typewriter Ribbon, you want a fried egg? I'll give you a fried egg!"

He got off his bike holding a giant magnifying glass, and tilted it over the egg so it caught the sun directly. Before long the clear goo around the yolk turned white and began to bubble around the edge. The yolk looked drier too, maybe a little hard on top.

Wouldn't you know, though, that Miss Quinn drove up right then on her way to lunch, and when she saw three guys crouched there on the sidewalk, she pulled over.

At Rosemary Acres, you can't even plant a flower without the approval of the Landscape Committee. I sure didn't want Randall to get into trouble, so I did the only thing I could think of. I sat on the egg.

Danny and Randall stared at me, and then they turned to Miss Quinn, who had rolled down her car window.

"Hello, boys," she said.

"Hi," I said. I could feel the egg soaking into the seat of my shorts.

"Sitting here on a hot sidewalk on a hundred-degree day?" she asked, looking at me strangely. Randall, I noticed, had slipped the magnifying glass into his hip pocket.

"Yep!" I said. "Just soaking up the old sun!" That didn't make a bit of sense because Danny and I already had deep tans. We were almost as dark as Randall, who's naturally brown.

Miss Quinn looked from one of us to the other. "The pool would feel pretty good on a hot afternoon," she suggested.

"Oh, we'll get there," said Danny. "We like to get real, real hot first, and then go swimming."

"Like to *fry*, almost!" put in Randall, grinning.

"Well, have fun," Miss Quinn said finally, and drove off.

We waited till she was around the corner, then burst out laughing. I leaned forward on my hands and knees while Danny peeled the egg off my rear end.

"What are you going to tell your mom about those pants?" Randall asked.

"I'll tell her I was out here hatching an egg," I said, and we guffawed some more.

Randall rode along beside us as we walked back to our house, and the three of us sprawled under the one decent tree in the development, which happens to be right outside my bedroom window. Paul Bremmer came by just then, still sweating from shooting baskets, and he stretched out on the grass, too. That guy'll shoot baskets in snow or rain or sun—it doesn't matter. He's a demon when it comes to basketball. Mom says it's probably the way he keeps his anger in check.

Then, of course, Mickey Harris saw us there on her way to the pool, so she stopped by—Mickey and Danny are both twelve—and wherever Mickey goes, she's got her nerdy stepbrother Norman with her, so the whole gang was there when Mom got back from the store.

"Well, if it isn't the desert rats," Mom said, laughing. She has light curly hair, not black and wavy like mine and Danny's, and she's got a smile that takes up half her face. "You all look like you crawled across the desert and lay down to die, you're so hot. Want some lemon-ade?"

We said yes, and after she went inside, Danny said, "I sort of like that–the Desert Rats."

"Yeah, the Rats," said Paul. "We're a pack. You know, we stick together."

Randall was lying on his back, arms behind his head, staring up through the leaves at the sky. "We have to," he said. "We're the only guys our age in the whole development."

"*Ahem!*" said Mickey.

"You included," said Randall.

"Am I included?" piped up Norman.

"Unfortunately," said Paul.

I liked the idea of it, too. Sort of a club, I mean. A gang, a group. All for one and one for all–that kind of stuff. Paul Bremer even sticking up for me, maybe.

"Danny's Desert Rats," I said proudly.

And that's the way it came about–what we started calling ourselves: Danny's Desert Rats, or just Rats for short.

Bonkers

The "sexy babe's" name was Diane Clark, and Mom said if she ever heard us call her "sexy babe" again, we could forget the ten dollars the woman was going to pay us; she wouldn't let us take it.

Danny and I hung around the doorway.

"Is it an insult to call a woman sexy?" Danny asked. He really wanted to know. We both did, and there's no dad around to ask.

Mom thought about it. "Not exactly, but 'sexy babe' implies that . . . well, that she's a baby, not a woman. That she has to be taken care of. That it's her body men admire."

Danny shrugged. "So why is it an insult to want to take care of a woman and admire her body?"

Now it was Mom who seemed confused.

"Well, when you put those two words together, they make her sound like . . . like a man's plaything, as though she was a . . . a *pleasure* machine!"

A *pleasure machine?* Boy, I'd never heard that before. I didn't think it would ever occur to me in a million years to call a girl a "pleasure machine." *Hi, Mickey, you pleasure machine, you!* Anyway, Mom said we could go get the key from Diane Clark if we called her "Miss Clark," so we walked across the street and rang the bell.

I didn't think it was polite to stare at her legs when she answered, but I knew it wasn't polite to stare at her breasts, either. I didn't know *what* it was polite to look at, so I concentrated on her nose, and that seemed to work. I made a mental note that if I ever didn't know what to look at on a girl, I should stare at her nose.

"Okay," she said, "let me show you what to do." We followed her into the dining room. There was a bay window, filled with plants, along one wall. "The cactus," she said, "won't need watering at all. The others should be watered once while I'm gone, but only if the soil feels dry to the touch. The fern up in my bedroom, though, needs watering every other day, sometimes every day in hot weather. It just soaks the water up. And it loves to be misted." She pointed to the spray bottle.

We nodded.

"Here's the key to the house, here's the key to my mailbox. Just pick up my mail every day and leave it here on the dining-room table. That's all you have to do. And keep on eye on the place. You know, if you see anyone hanging around at night, call security."

"Okay," said Danny. "We've got it."

"Have a good time on your vacation, Miss Babe," I said, and stopped, my mouth open.

"What?" the woman said.

"I mean, Diane. No, I mean . . ."

"Clark," said Danny. "He meant Miss Clark."

"Yeah, I will," she said.

We took the keys and walked back across the street.

"Jerk!" Danny said, elbowing me.

"Well, I got mixed up."

We laughed.

Paul couldn't believe we were going to be in the sexy babe's . . . I mean, Miss Clark's . . . house every day.

"What's it like?" he asked.

I shrugged. "Just a house," I said.

"Will you let me come with you sometime and look around?"

"No, Mom would have a fit," Danny told him.

Paul kept after us, though. "Aren't we a club?" he kept saying. "Aren't we a team?" About the only time he's not moody is when we're talking about girls. Women, in this case. And the next day, just before we went to get Miss Clark's mail, Paul called.

"Listen, you guys . . ." he said, and his voice was low and strange.

"We *can't*, Paul!" I said. "Mom knows we're going over there and she'd find out. Besides, you—"

"Not that!" said Paul. "You guys gotta come over here right now. Something's happened."

"What?" I asked.

11

"Come *over!*" Paul said, and hung up.

I grabbed Danny's arm. "We can take care of the plants later. Something's going on at Paul's."

Danny looked at me. "Good or bad?"

"He didn't tell me. He just said to come." He didn't say only Danny, either. He said, "You guys." I really liked being a member of the Desert Rats.

We don't know the Bremmers too well. Paul and his dad aren't the easiest people in the world to talk to. Mr. Bremmer clams up when we're around. Never smiles. When he's not at work, he shuts himself up in the house; Paul closes up inside himself sometimes, too.

"Do you suppose Mr. Bremmer jumped out a window or something? Just decided to end it all because his wife's dead?" I asked Danny. "Paul sure sounded serious."

"I don't think anyone would be dumb enough to jump from a second-story window," Danny said.

I tried to figure it out. "What I don't understand is, if Mr. Bremmer's sad because his wife died, why doesn't he just get another wife?"

"Life isn't that easy," Danny said, as if he understands any more than I do. "Why don't we get another dad? Things don't work that way." Danny can get pretty serious sometimes. I know he thinks about Mom a lot— wonders if she's happy. I guess we both hate our dad's guts for leaving the family and going off with his graduate assistant. At the same time, though, I want him back. I want things to be like they were a long time ago, but Danny says that will never happen.

Paul lives on the next street. When we got there we ran up the steps of their town house. Mr. Bremmer's car was gone, and we figured maybe he just took off. Left the house and everything to Paul.

The door opened, and Paul pulled us inside and shut it quickly behind us. I'd never seen him look the way he did then. Excited and mysterious.

"Guess what?" he said.

Danny and I just stood there.

Paul pointed to the living room, and there on the sofa was a cat, a yellow cat with green eyes.

"Whose is it?" I asked.

"Mine!" said Paul.

"Rosemary Acres doesn't allow pets!" I said.

"I know, but he came *back*!"

"This is the same cat that . . . ?"

"Yeah!" Paul was grinning now. "We gave him to that family in Aurora."

"They brought him back?" I asked.

"No! He must have run away! That's fifteen miles off, and somehow he found his way back. I heard him meowing outside the door about an hour ago, and thought it was some stray. At first I hardly recognized him, but he sure knew me." Paul smiled at the cat.

"Have you called the family in Aurora and told them?"

"I don't even remember their name. Dad might, I suppose. They probably won't call us, 'cause they wouldn't guess he'd find his way back here in a million years."

We walked over to the couch and looked at the cat.

He was thin and bedraggled and seemed exhausted, licking himself all over with half-closed eyes.

"What are you going to do?" Danny asked.

"I know one thing," said Paul determinedly. "I'm not going to give him up."

"Wow!" I breathed.

"Where's your dad?"

"Consulting job. He'll be back tonight." And then Paul looked us right in the eyes. "You guys have to help me hide him. The Desert Rats have got to come through."

We stared at Paul.

"*How?*" asked Danny.

"He'll meow!" I said.

"Not if he's here with me. He was always a pretty quiet cat that way."

"He'll want to go out," I said.

Paul shook his head. "He was a house cat. We'd let him out and he'd just hang around the steps. Sort of a scaredy-cat, if you want the truth. That's why it's so weird he got back here all by himself. He must have been so scared . . . the highways and everything." Paul sat down on the couch and stroked the cat's head.

"But he'll . . . you know . . . when a female cat comes around, he'll . . ." I began.

"He's been neutered," said Paul.

"Ouch!" Danny said, and doubled over with a phantom pain.

Both Danny and I were staring at the cat, though. He was half-sitting now, with one leg in the air, and licking himself where, if he were a kid, he couldn't reach.

"But he's got balls!" Danny protested.

"Well, sort of," Paul explained. "The vet says he always leaves a little something so the cat won't know the difference, but he removes all the important stuff. In other words, he can't be a father. More important, I guess, he won't ever want to."

You know what I was thinking just then? I was wondering if men who don't want to be fathers could have that little operation done. Then they wouldn't ever have kids they didn't want to spend time with.

"If he never has to go out and he never makes any noise, who will know?" I asked. "What do you need us for?"

Paul gently massaged behind his cat's ears. "Well, somehow I've got to get bags of kitty litter and cat food into the house without anyone seeing, and be careful when I throw stuff out. I guess that's easy enough. But what if Dad and I go on a trip or something? What happens then?"

"We'll think of something," said Danny.

He and I sat down on the floor by the couch to pet the cat, too. The yellow cat gave our hands a sniff to see if there was any trace of dog, I guess, and then started this deep rattly purr that sounded like a coffee percolator.

"What's his name?" I asked.

Paul grinned. "Bonkers."

"Bonkers?"

"When he was little, he'd chase his tail and go absolutely nuts. 'He's going bonkers,' Mom said the first day we had him, so that's what we called him after that."

And then Paul said, in this really soft voice, "He was actually Mom's cat; she was the one who chose him, and he loved her best. I'm not giving him away again, no matter what."

And Danny and I knew that, rules or no rules, Paul deserved that cat.

More About Mickey

Paul decided that only four of the Rats should know about Bonkers to begin with–Paul, Danny, Mickey, and me. Norman we couldn't trust, and we weren't so sure about Randall. His folks are pretty strict, and the last thing in the world they'd want is Randall getting in trouble over a cat. Randall wouldn't squeal on us, but they might. Man, I was glad that Paul let me in on it.

"Whoever sees Mickey first, ask if she'd be willing to help hide a cat," Paul said when we left his place.

"Call her," I suggested.

"Nah," said Danny.

Danny and Paul are weird that way. They think about Mickey and talk about Mickey, but will they call her? No. They'll ride by her house a dozen times on their bikes or sit at the pool for two solid hours, just waiting for her to show up. But they won't dial her number.

"I'm not going to be like that when I'm twelve," I told Danny once. "If I want to ask a girl something, I'll just ask her. If I want to see her, I'll walk up to her house and ring the bell."

"Yeah, sure," said Danny.

I didn't figure we had anything to worry about with Mickey anyway. Girls love warm, cuddly things, and I could just see her wrapping Bonkers in a blanket and smuggling him up to her room. I remembered the way she'd made a cradle out of her skirt there on her steps once, and rocked Gus, her baby brother. Half brother, I guess you'd call him, because they had different fathers. She reminds me a little of Aunt Cis (Aunt Cecelia, really), who will rescue any creature that comes along, even a mouse.

We didn't see Mickey the rest of the afternoon, but when Danny and I went to the pool around five, there she was, stretched out on her stomach on a vinyl deck chair, wearing her green bikini. Norman was sitting in the wading pool with a mask and snorkel on. Only Norman the Nerd would go snorkeling in eighteen inches of water.

This was our chance, so Danny and I crowded onto the deck chair next to Mickey. A large woman was in the chair on the other side of her, so we had to be careful what we said. We couldn't come right out and tell her about Bonkers.

"Hi, Mickey," I said, nudging Danny to scoot over, because I was practically falling off the end.

"Hi, Scarlino," she said, without even turning her head. I guess she recognized my voice. Sometimes she calls me T.R., and sometimes she calls me by our last name, Scarlino, and when she's talking about Danny and me together, she calls us the Scarlino brothers, the way Paul does. Paul thinks it's cool, because it makes us sound like the Mafia or something, but Danny and I just like being Italian. Well, half-Italian, anyway. Mom's Irish.

Danny and I sat there on the deck chair waiting for Mickey to sit up or turn over. She has short legs and a long dark ponytail, only this time she didn't have her hair tied back; it hung loose around her shoulders like a waterfall.

Finally Danny asked, "Have you seen Paul yet?"

Mickey turned over and shielded her eyes with one hand. "No. Why would I see Paul?"

Danny shrugged. "I just thought maybe he would have called you or something."

Over in the wading pool, Norman was making bubbling noises. He was lowering his head just enough to put the tube underwater, then blowing. Any minute he would see us and come over. I knew we had to act fast.

"Have you ever had any pets?" I asked.

Mickey opened one eye and looked at me. "We had a dog once—a springer spaniel. I really loved that dog. Then she got hit by a car and we had to put her to sleep."

"That's too bad," I said.

Mickey squinted off into the distance. "Yeah. The thing about Roxie, when you were sad, she was sad with you. When you were happy, she'd bounce around, ready to do anything you wanted."

I wondered if that's the way it was with Paul and his cat; they were both missing Paul's mom. I looked at the woman sitting on the other side of Mickey—was she reading or listening?

"Norman had a bird once," Mickey went on, "but he was cleaning out its cage and it flew out the front door and never came back."

"I wouldn't either," I said. "If I was a bird and got away, I sure wouldn't come back." Especially to Norman.

"How about cats?" asked Danny.

"I hate cats," said Mickey, and closed her eyes again.

Danny and I looked at each other. How could she hate cats? How could a girl who loved dogs and baby brothers not like cats?

"Why?" I bleated.

"Because they won't go for walks with you, they won't come when you call them, and they do exactly as they please. The last thing in this world I'd want is a cat."

"Even a tiny little kitten?" I asked.

"*Especially* a tiny little kitten," said Mickey. She pointed to the space above her lip. "See that scar? Well, I guess you'd have to be awfully close to see it, but I was holding a kitten once, and it scratched me good."

I was just about to lean in closer when Danny beat me to it. He was so close to Mickey he could have kissed her. I decided I didn't want to kiss a girl who hated cats.

"You mean," I said at last, "that if a stray cat came to your door and meowed, you wouldn't even feed it?"

The big woman on the other side of Mickey put down her magazine and looked our way. "No pets allowed at Rosemary Acres," she said.

"Right," said Danny. "Of course not. Who wants pets?"

"Well, *that's* settled, then!" said Mickey, and sat up. She swung her legs over the side of the deck chair. "Last one in the pool is a rotten banana," she called. She ran to the edge and dived in.

Danny and I looked at each other, shrugged, and followed.

We played underwater tag for a while. I swam right between a guy's legs who was standing at the shallow end, and I don't think he even knew it.

Danny kept swimming closer and closer to Mickey's face, and I wondered whether he was playing tag or trying to kiss her. I didn't know if he'd ever kissed a girl or not. Maybe it's easier to kiss underwater. You could always say it was an accident.

I watched the bubbles coming up out of Mickey's mouth, and it seemed to me I could hear a little kitten mewing. Could she be making those noises? The more I thought about it, the more sure I was there really *was* a cat crying somewhere. The next time I surfaced for air, I realized that the mewing sound was Norman, standing by the side of the pool whining. His snorkel, mask, and fins dangled from one hand, and his voice was like a siren.

"Mick-ey!" he whined. "I'm hun-gry!"

"Go eat your socks, Norman," I said.

"What?"

"Quit whining," I told him.

"I hardly had any lunch!" he complained.

"So go make yourself a sandwich!" Jeez, what a revolting kid. I wondered if I was like that when I was eight.

"It's almost dinner time!" he wailed.

"So go eat dinner!"

"Mickey's supposed to be taking care of me!"

Maybe *that's* why Mickey didn't like cats, I decided. They sounded too much like Norman. I wished we didn't have to include him in the Desert Rats, but if we wanted Mickey as a member, we had to take her brother, too.

We called Paul later and told him what Mickey had said.

"How could anyone not like cats?" asked Paul.

"Beats me," Danny told him. "How's Bonkers doing? Does your dad know yet?"

"Yeah. He's glad to see him, too. He says that any cat who walks fifteen miles deserves to stay, but just don't let the neighbors know."

"Yeah, right," said Danny.

Number Four

Did you water Diane Clark's plants?" Mom asked after dinner, and we realized we hadn't done that yet.

"We're going over right now," Danny told her.

"Don't touch anything else in her house besides her plants," Mom said.

Danny and I looked at each other. How do moms *do* that? How do they know what's way back in your mind before you've even thought of it yourself?

"What would we touch?" asked Danny, his hand on the doorknob.

"You know exactly what I mean," said Mom. "No horsing around."

We crossed the street, walked to the corner, and got the mail from Miss Clark's box, then went to her town house, and Danny put the key in the lock. I took a good look around this time. Her house is the same as ours except everything's backwards. Her stairs are on the right side of the hallway, ours are on the left—stuff like that.

But while Mom has plants everywhere, hanging from the ceiling of every room, practically, Miss Clark had beads. Curtains of beads, I mean. At the windows, in the doorway between her dining room and kitchen. Her lampshades had beads, too, and everything was a different color. Nothing matched. It wasn't supposed to, I guess. Sort of like walking in Woolworth's at Christmas.

"Okay," said Danny, looking around. "Get the watering can from the kitchen, T.R. I don't think we need to do anything to the plants here in the dining room, but we'll give that fern upstairs a long drink."

I followed him with the watering can and a paper towel to mop up anything we spilled. The fern was so large it took up one whole corner of the bedroom and almost covered the window. We let the water run out of the can slowly so it had a chance to sink down into the soil. Then we stood on the rug in the middle of Diane Clark's bedroom and looked around. There were more beads at the window in place of curtains, but otherwise it looked like an ordinary bedroom to me.

"Boy," I said, "she sure does have a lot of drawers in her dressers; she sure must have a lot of underwear."

"Yeah," Danny said again.

"Danny," I said. "There was this guy at school whose sister was getting married. He told us that she bought a bunch of fancy underwear, including a lace garter belt, and he laughed. What's a garter belt?"

"Oh, some kind of underwear," Danny said. "It's what women wear when they want to look sexy."

I tried to imagine what kind of a belt would look sexy.

"If you ever see one, point it out to me," I said.

Women sure are complicated, I thought. A guy puts on his socks and shorts and shirt and pants, but a woman puts on her slip and stockings and panties and bra and garter belt and I don't know what all. Not Mom, though. She wears a T-shirt and jeans whenever she can.

We locked the door after us when we left and put the key in the bowl on our dining-room table.

"We're going over to Paul's, Mom," Danny called.

"Okay. When it gets dark, either come home or call. Don't make me worry about you," she said.

Paul's dad was there, and he actually smiled at us. It was the first time we'd ever seen him smile.

"You guys in on the plot?" he asked.

"Yeah." Danny grinned. "We want Paul to keep the cat."

"Well, so do I, but I don't know what we'll do when management finds out," said Mr. Bremmer.

Paul came thumping down the stairs just then with Bonkers in his arms. "We've got problems, Dad," he said. "You know that bay window in the upstairs hall? Bonkers keeps jumping up on the window ledge. The other windows in the house don't have sills, but if he sits up there, people can see him from all over the neighborhood."

"Pull the blind, then," said Mr. Bremmer.

"I tried. He crawls right between the window and the blind. He likes to look out."

"Back a chair up against the window ledge."

"I did. He just jumps over."

Mr. Bremmer gave a sigh. "We can't cat-proof the whole house, Paul."

"But what'll we do? Miss Quinn drives around just

looking for stuff like this. Nothing would make her happier than to tell us we had twenty-four hours to get rid of Bonkers."

"He's right," said Danny. "Quinn sure picks up on stuff like this."

"Nothing would make Quinn happier than drowning Bonkers in Lake Tarragon," I said.

We like Miss Quinn about as much as we like dog poop.

"Well, I'm stumped," said Mr. Bremmer.

Danny looked at me. I looked at Danny.

"We gotta tell Randall," I said.

Danny stayed at Paul's, but I pedaled over to Randall's and dropped my bike on their lawn.

I figured everybody would be through eating by now, but the Hayeses were finishing up dinner outside on the patio. Mrs. Hayes had a big bowl of fresh peaches, and she'd just come outside with a half gallon of ice cream and was dipping it up for desert.

"Hey, Tie Rack!" Randall called.

"We're having *peaches*!" his little sister said.

"How did you know we were having ice cream and peaches, T.R.?" Randall's mother teased. "Here's a bowl. Help yourself."

I was thinking how if we had taken this town house, the one we looked at first, maybe *we* would be sitting out here on the patio eating peaches and ice cream like the Hayeses. But I knew that even if we *had* taken it, and we were eating ice cream on the patio, it wouldn't be like the Hayeses, because there's a dad in that family and there's not one in ours. Not living with us, anyway.

Mr. Hayes took a spoonful of his ice cream and dropped it in his coffee. He stirred until the coffee was almost the color of his hand.

"Is your family going to go on a vacation before summer's over?" he asked me.

"Naw, I don't think so," I said, accidentally letting one of the peach slices slip through my teeth. It slid down my throat unchewed. "We may drive back to Chicago again to see Aunt Cis before school starts, but Mom says just moving out here will have to be our adventure this year. What about you?"

"We'll probably just hit the parks, maybe drive down to Starved Rock some weekend," Mr. Hayes told me.

What I wanted, of course, was to get Randall away where I could tell him about Paul's cat, but you can't very well sit down with a family on their patio, and as soon as you've eaten dessert, excuse yourself.

So I had to listen to Leah's jokes and help clean off the table, and finally, when I followed Randall inside to put the ice cream away, I said, "I've got to talk to you in private. It's important!"

Randall looked over at me as he opened the freezer door. "I'll bet!" he said. "You guys spying on Mickey again?"

"No. She's got nothing to do with it."

"Well, come on up to my room."

We went upstairs. Leah's bedroom, at the top, had racing car wallpaper. Hers was the smallest bedroom, the room I would have got if we'd taken this house. Randall's room didn't look like a bedroom at all. There were shoe boxes, cigar boxes, and old trays sitting on every bit of open space. Each one was filled with wire, bolts and nuts, batteries, pliers, aluminum foil, screening, cardboard, thumbtacks, paper plates, tubes, wheels, string, gears, ropes . . .

"Junkyard!" I said.

"Hey, Tie Rack, don't knock it," said Randall. "You ever see Thomas Edison's lab?"

"The guy who invented the lightbulb? Of course not. He's dead."

"I know, but I'll bet his lab was as messy as this."

My mom's a teacher, and she says that some teacher's sure going to be lucky this fall to have Randall in her class, 'cause his mind never stops whirring. I wished I was a year older so Randall and I could be in the same room.

"What are you inventing this time?" I asked.

"What do you need?"

My heart beat a little faster. "It's a secret operation, and you're the only one we can trust."

Randall immediately looked suspicious. "Is this Paul guy in on it, too? My dad says Paul Bremmer's bad news."

"It's something to do with the Desert Rats," I told him. "Listen, Randall, do you like animals?"

"What kind of animals?" He was looking more suspicious by the minute.

"Pets, I mean. Dogs and cats."

"Sure."

"What would you say if I told you some guy gave his cat away and the cat walked fifteen miles to come back to his master again."

"I'd say the dude should keep the cat."

"That's what I think," I said, and explained why Paul had to give Bonkers away in the first place. How all the other Desert Rats were getting to like Rosemary Acres except Paul, and how the cat could be the thing to turn him around–that it used to belong to his mom. Maybe having the cat back was like having a little bit of his mom there, too, I said.

Randall listened. "So what's it have to do with me?"

"The cat keeps jumping up on the window ledge in their hall, and someone's going to see him. Paul's tried everything. Can you think of a way to keep the cat off the ledge?"

Giving Randall Hayes an idea is like dropping money in a Coke machine. You can almost hear his wheels grinding away, his mind clicking like a computer.

"Leave it to me," he said.

Shark

I let the secret out. I didn't mean to at all. I hadn't even known I was going to do it! But the phone rang while Mom was in the tub that night and Danny was playing a computer game, so I was the one who answered.

"T.R.!" came Grandma Flora's voice. Flora from Florida, Mom calls her, though she was actually born in Italy. She's Dad's mom, but she's our grandma same as always. She says she loves her son (Dad), but she doesn't love what he did (left us, I mean). She's not like the Italian grandmothers you see on jars of spaghetti sauce, though. She's small and classy-looking and wears her silver-black hair cut short.

"So what you do these days, T.R., and don' you keep any secrets from me," she began. That's the way she is. Right to the point.

"Oh, same as always," I said. "We're waiting for school to start."

"I'm no dumb-dumb," she said. "Two brothers, ten and twelve, don' spend August waiting for school."

"Well, sure, we've got a lot to do. Same old stuff we always do," I told her.

"You still got friends, don' you? The girl, this Mickey?"

"Yeah, but we haven't seen much of her the last couple of days because . . ." I stopped.

"Danny has a girlfriend for one month and already they're enemies?"

"No, because . . . well, nothing."

"And this Paul boy?"

"Well, we see him a lot, but . . ." I stopped again. It is one hundred percent impossible to keep a secret from Grandma Flora, and when she smells a secret, you're gone.

"So what's happened, T.R.?" she said. "You might as well tell me. Something going on between Paul and Mickey now?"

"No. You've got it all wrong. Mickey's not even in on it!" I said.

"Aha! On what?"

"Nothing!"

"T.R., I got nothing to do but sit here on my porch in Florida with my phone in my lap, so you might as well tell me."

I sighed. "Can you keep a secret?"

"Is the Pope Catholic?"

"Yeah, but I bet you'll tell Mom."

"You're right. I don' keep secrets from your mother."

"Then I can't tell you."

"I ask you this, T.R. Is this secret—somebody going to get hurt?"

"No."

"Something going to be destroyed?"

"No."

"Are you and Danny going to end up in jail?"

"No."

"Then I keep your secret, even from your mother. Now tell me."

So I told her about Paul's cat.

"You do the right thing!" she said. "Of *course* Paul should keep that cat. It's like children. You don' never give up on them."

"Well, that's sort of the way we figured it," I told her.

She talked to Danny after that, and then, after Mom got out of the tub, to her. But Grandma Flora kept her word. She didn't mention to either one of them that she knew about Bonkers.

You'd think, though, that with a cat just waiting to be discovered, Paul and Danny would try not to rock the boat. I mean, that they'd lie low and not do anything to get in trouble. Wrong.

That's what's so hard about being Danny's brother. I have to keep my eye on him all the time, because when you're twelve, I guess, you just do dumb things. When I'm twelve, Danny will be fourteen, and maybe he'll keep an eye on me then, but for now, it's me looking out for Danny.

I don't mind exactly. What ticks me off is when Danny and Paul do stuff without letting me in on it.

And it happened again the next day in the Rosemary Acres pool.

I knew they had plans when I noticed the way Paul was carrying his towel. It was wrapped around something big and flat. He tried to disguise it by carrying it under his arm, but nobody has a towel as stiff as a stop sign.

"What's in the towel?" I asked.

"Just a towel," says Paul, like I'm some moron.

"Yeah, sure," I said, and looked at Danny, only he was taking off his shoes.

I also noticed they didn't go over to talk to Mickey, who was lying on her towel with her eyes closed.

It was about five thirty in the afternoon and the pool was pretty full. There were a lot of fathers home from work early to get in a swim before dinner, and a lot of younger kids around seven or eight horsing around in the water, waiting to be called home. I decided not even to go in the water, just to sit on a deck chair and see what Danny and Paul were up to.

They were sitting on the edge of the pool now, but at the deep end, and Paul still had his towel beside him. They were whispering, and just when the pool looked about as crowded as it could get, Danny slipped into the water. He had his fingers closed around something small, and he swam out to the middle. Then Paul pulled his towel off something flat and gray, and slid into the water.

As I watched, Paul suddenly ducked down under the surface and I saw this big gray shark fin moving slowly through the water.

Danny began to yell: "Shark! Shark!"

People stared at him, then turned around to look at the shark fin. Some kid screamed. Then somebody else screamed.

The shark fin got up to Danny, and suddenly arms and legs were tossing around, and the water began to turn red. I knew right off that Danny had slipped into the water with a little bottle of Mom's red food-dye.

Now lots of people were yelling and swimming toward the sides. The lifeguard stood up and blew his whistle like mad. Mothers were pulling their kids out of the pool while fathers stayed at the edge, wiping water out of their eyes, trying to figure out what the heck was going on.

A moment later, Paul was back in his corner, the artificial shark fin down under the water between his knees, as though he could hide it, and Danny was swimming away, trying to pretend that a shark had bitten his arm.

The lifeguard sure didn't think it was funny. He yelled at Danny and Paul to get out of the pool, and said they were barred for the rest of the week.

"Nice going, Danny," I muttered. Jeez, what a dumb thing to do!

Mickey, though, thought it was funny. As soon as Danny yelled, "Shark!" she'd sat up and watched the whole thing.

"You've got a wild-and-crazy brother," she said to me, coming over.

"That's 'cause he hangs around with wild-and-crazy Paul," I told her. We both sat down on the edge of the pool.

Norm came running.

"Where'd Paul get that fin?" he asked. "You think he'd let me have it sometime?"

"Sure. Use it in the wading pool," I said. "Get yourself barred for life." That made Mickey laugh. I like to make her laugh. She's got nice teeth. We were sitting so close that her leg was almost touching mine. She's got freckles not only on her face but over her whole body as far as you can see. I'll bet she even has freckles on her butt.

"I haven't seen Paul and Danny around much lately," she said. "What are those guys up to these days?"

"Well, it's . . . sort of a secret," I said, in a whisper that Norman the Nerd couldn't hear.

I was sorry as soon as I'd said it, 'cause Mickey acted as though she'd been slapped. She drew away from me and said, "I thought *I* was one of the Desert Rats. I thought Paul said we'd stick together. How come *I'm* not in on this secret?"

I tried to think what Danny would want me to say. He sure wouldn't want me to make Mickey mad at him. I glanced again at Norm, so Mickey said, "Hey, Norm, if you want a Popsicle before we go, get it now. Last chance."

"Okay," said Norm.

"And eat it over at the tables, remember."

Mickey can get rid of Norm as easily as ice cream in a bowl.

"Now," she said, leaning toward me and looking right into my eyes. I swallowed.

"No matter how much you hate cats, Mickey, you've got to keep a secret."

"Cats?"

"You promise?"

"Sure. What do cats have to do with it?"

I told her about Bonkers.

Her eyes went all crinkly at the corners. "Poor kitty!" she said. "Fifteen miles! Paul's *got* to keep him, of course! What else could he do?"

If I'd had the nerve, I would have put my arms around Mickey and kissed her. I'll bet Danny would have.

"And the Desert Rats have to help hide it," I told her.

"You can count me in," said Mickey.

I could hardly wait to get back and tell Danny, but he must have gone over to Paul's, because no one was there when I got home. I could see Mom way back in the yard, and the phone was ringing. I wondered if the lifeguard had reported Danny to Miss Quinn, and hoped it wasn't her calling to tell Mom what Danny had done in the pool.

I lifted the receiver. It was Aunt Mavis. On Mom's side of the family there's Grandpa Gil, up in Wisconsin; then Mavis and her husband, Uncle Floyd, in Forest Park. Then Mom, and then Keith, who goes to Northwestern.

"T.R.?" Aunt Mavis said anxiously. "I've been ringing and ringing. Where is everyone?"

I don't know why I do it. For the same reason Paul and Danny played that trick in the pool, I guess. But I heard myself saying, "There was a horrible accident in the pool, Aunt Mave, and I just got back. Danny was in the deep end, and the next thing I knew, he was kicking and screaming, and there was blood all over the place!"

"Oh my God!" cried Aunt Mavis. "What happened?"

"Shark," I said.

There was a long, long pause.

"T.R., put your mother on right this minute. I mean it!" she said, and she didn't seem very worried about Danny.

Randall's
Invention

Randall came through. He made this mat, see, covered with wire mesh connected to this humongous battery, and rigged it so it would give off a shock if you touched it. There was just enough current to give your hand a real buzz, and you'd want to jerk it away quick. He brought it over to Paul's to try out. The idea was to set it on the window ledge in the upstairs hall, so that when Bonkers jumped up to see out, he'd get a shock and never want to go near the window again.

"There's just one problem," said Randall. "I don't know how much current it takes to kill a cat."

Paul and Danny and I simply stared. Randall had made an invention that would keep Bonkers off the window ledge, but might kill him if he tried?

"Are you crazy?" said Paul.

We were all standing in the upstairs hallway of the Bremmers' town house. Paul's dad was at work. Randall had placed the mat on the window ledge, connected the wires, and we'd all taken turns putting our hands on the wire mesh to feel the buzz. But *nobody* was willing to set Bonkers on it and watch him fry.

The doorbell rang and we looked at each other.

"Trou-ble!" said Randall.

"Bet it's Quinn," said Danny. "Go answer, T.R., and tell her we're not here."

"Yeah, sure! So what am *I* doing in Paul's house, then?"

"House-sitting," said Paul. "The Bremmers aren't home, see, and you're house-sitting."

I always get stuck with things like this just because Paul and Danny wanted to play shark in the pool, I thought as I clumped downstairs. Why couldn't Paul answer his own stupid door? They want to make Quinn mad at them, that's their worry, not mine.

I felt like going back upstairs and telling them off, but I didn't. I opened the front door, and there stood Mickey.

"Saw your bikes out front and figured you were here," she said. "The Desert Rats aren't having a meeting without me, are they?"

"Of course not!" I said, glad to see her. "Come on in. We're trying out Randall's invention."

Mickey followed me up the stairs.

I'd already told Danny that Mickey knew about Bonkers, but Paul and Randall didn't know, and when Paul tried to hide the cat behind him, Mickey said, "Relax. I know all about your kitty. Just don't make me hold him, okay?" She pointed to the little place above her lip. "Cat scratch," she said. "So what do we have here?" She looked at the mat, the battery, and the wires. "What are you trying to do, Randall? Electrocute him?"

"What we need," said Randall, "is somebody to test the cat."

"Don't look at me," said Mickey. "I just got here."

"Okay, here's what we'll do," said Randall. "Put a pile of towels on the mat, and set the cat on top. If he doesn't get a shock and jump off, we'll keep removing towels one by one, till we get to the place where he gets a shock but not enough to hurt him."

Paul got a stack of towels and put Bonkers on top. The cat began to purr and immediately pawed at the towels, ready to bed down.

"Okay, take one away," said Randall.

Paul lifted up Bonkers and Danny pulled out one of the towels from the stack. Bonkers went back on the towels again. This time he sat down and yawned.

"Take away another one," said Randall.

We kept on until there were only two towels left. We held our breath when we put Bonkers back again. He didn't seem to be suffering, just looked bored. Bonkers went over to the window and tried to nose his way behind the shade.

Paul picked him up and Danny pulled out one of the two remaining towels.

Nobody said a word when Paul slowly set the cat down paws first on the mat with just one towel on it. Bonkers looked down and walked a little, then jumped off, but we couldn't tell if he was feeling anything or not.

Finally Paul picked up Bonkers and Danny removed the last towel.

"You sure we ought to do this?" I asked.

"What's our choice?" asked Danny.

Mickey reached toward the connecting wire, ready to yank it out, if necessary.

Paul took a deep breath. We all watched as he lowered Bonkers over the mat. Any minute, I thought, we'd hear a yowl and see him rise to the ceiling, his fur standing on end.

Bonkers's paws hit the mat. Paul let go and the cat instantly jumped off, shaking his paws after he landed. We cheered. Paul set him on the mat again, and this time Bonkers hissed at him before he jumped.

"You *did* it, Randall!" Danny said. "Nice going, man!"

"Thanks a lot!" said Paul. "You want a Coke, Randall? Ice cream or something?"

"We *all* do!" said Mickey. "Let's celebrate."

Paul got out some root beer and straws, then ice cream, and the Desert Rats sat around his kitchen making root beer floats. Every time the root beer got low, we added more. Then we'd run out of ice cream and dip up some more of that. We figured we could probably make our floats last all afternoon at this speed.

It was fun having just the five of us together, without Nerdy Norman around. I was starting to feel really good about being at Rosemary Acres, even though Danny and I had left a whole bunch of friends back in the city. I was finally a part of Danny's crowd, really one of the guys, I thought. But then I had to blow it.

Randall had walked over to the sink to get a drink of water, and I noticed that he had a carpenter's belt slung low over his hips with extra wire hanging from it, pliers, a screwdriver, and stuff.

"Hey, Randall," I said. "What are you wearing? Your garter belt?" And laughed.

Randall spun around. "What are you talking about?"

"What do you know about garter belts, T.R.?" Paul guffawed.

"Don't mind him," said Danny. "T.R.'s got this thing about garter belts lately." I could feel my face burning red. Danny doesn't usually say things like that, but he was showing off in front of the Rats.

"Boy, you really *are* a weirdo!" Mickey said to me, and as much as I'd liked her before, I didn't like her now.

"It was a joke," I said quickly. "Forget it."

But Paul said, "You want to see a garter belt, T.R., I'll bet the sexy babe has plenty."

"Who's the sexy babe?" asked Randall.

"Diane Clark," Danny told him. "We're taking in her mail and watering her plants while she's gone. And she's got a zillion drawers in her bedroom."

"This is a dumb conversation if I ever heard one," said Mickey. She reached the root beer in the bottom of her glass, sucked it up, then wiped her hand across her mouth. "I've got to get home and sit Gus while Mom goes shopping," she said. "See you later."

We hung around Paul's for a while, but as Danny and I rode home on our bikes, he said, "That was a really stupid thing to say to Randall, T.R."

"It was a joke!" I bleated again. "So I'm a piece of manure. So what?" I guess I was feeling a little bit angry, too.

"Well, if you really want to know about garter belts and stuff, ask Mom," said Danny.

So I did. At dinner that night, I told Mom that I'd always wondered what a garter belt was, and did she wear one?

"A garter belt?" Mom threw back her head and laughed. "Those uncomfortable old things? The only women I know who wear garter belts are the models you see in magazines."

"What magazines?" I asked.

"Never mind," said Mom. "*Those* kinds of magazines we can do without."

Danny didn't say anything, but after dinner, when he and I were doing the dishes, he said, "Listen, T.R., I'll bet Diane Clark has some garter belts. If you really want to see what they look like, I don't think it would hurt to look in a couple of her drawers."

"She's going to be home in two days," I warned him.

"Then we'll take a quick look tomorrow, and I'll bet you anything we find one," said Danny.

I was beginning to wish I'd never brought the subject up. It was just that I like to *know* things. I don't want to be like a guy back in Chicago who didn't know what girls' periods were. He thought they were punctuation marks!

Big Mistake

The next day the mail was late. It didn't come till after lunch. But as soon as Mom came in from the corner holding a bunch of letters, Danny gave me the signal.

"We're going to get Miss Clark's mail, Mom," he said, taking the key from the bowl on the dining-room table.

"Um-hmm," she murmured distractedly, studying an envelope in her hand, and moved on into the living room.

Danny and I walked down to the bank of mailboxes on the corner and got the mail from Miss Clark's box. It was mostly bills, plus an envelope from Victoria's Secret, with a picture of a woman in a black nightgown on it.

Danny grinned as we walked back to Miss Clark's town house. "You know what Victoria's Secret is, don't you, T.R.?"

"How would I know her secret? I don't even know Victoria," I said.

He laughed. "It's a store that sells sexy clothes. They

probably have hundreds of garter belts, any color you want." I wouldn't know anything at all if it weren't for Danny.

He turned the key in the lock, and we put the mail on the table. The only plant that needed watering this time was the fern up in her bedroom, and we filled the watering can in the kitchen, then took it upstairs.

It took about ten seconds to water the fern, and then we looked around at the dresser drawers.

"All we'll do is check," said Danny.

He took the chest of drawers and I took the dresser. We carefully opened each drawer and looked in, then closed it again. Scarves, sweaters, stockings—nothing that looked like a belt to me. But when I got to the next drawer, I found a whole bunch of underpants.

"Hey, Danny!" I said.

He was standing on the other side of the room, and turned around. I pulled out the drawer and over-turned it on the bed, grinning. Some of the pants had lace around the legs, and some were lace all over. There were bikinis with big blue polka dots, and another pair of red, white, and blue stripes. I held up a pair of white satin pants with pink rosebuds and a tiny bow in front.

"Look at this!" Danny said, reaching out and lifting up a pair. They looked like curtains. You could see right through them! He whistled and we laughed some more. "Wait'll I tell Paul," said Danny.

"How about these?" I held up a pair that had paw prints all over them, as though Miss Clark had been lying on her stomach and a dog with muddy paws had walked right across her bottom. We yelped some more.

Then there was something I thought was a pair of pants, but when I held it up, I could see that it had a top, too. It was all one piece, like a bathing suit.

"That's a teddy," Danny said knowingly. "It has snaps at the bottom."

I checked, and sure enough, it had snaps. How did he know about stuff like that? I threw it across the bed at him and he threw it back. We laughed some more.

"Boys!"

Mom! She was coming up the stairs!

"What are you guys doing that's taking so long?" she called.

I grabbed the drawer and managed to get it back in the dresser, while Danny scooped up all the underpants and shoved them under the bed.

Mom came through the doorway just as we straightened up and stood like soldiers at attention.

"I thought you were watering plants," she said.

"We were," I gulped, and pointed to the watering can over by the fern. If Mom looked under the bed, we were dead ducks.

She glanced around. "Well, what are you doing on that side of the room, then? Come on home. You shouldn't be fooling around up here. Is there anything else that needs watering?"

"No," said Danny, picking up the can.

"Then let's go," she said, and waited till we were out of the bedroom before following us downstairs. I could see Danny's shoulders sag with relief.

Back home, we put the key in the bowl again.

"*That* was close!" Danny whispered, grinning.

"I didn't even hear her come in!" I whispered back. "We must have left the door unlocked." Then I added, "We still didn't find a garter belt."

"We've got one more chance tomorrow," Danny said. "We'll put the stuff back in the drawer and check the others. But we've got to remember to lock the door when we get inside!"

"Hey, guys," came Mom's voice from the living room, "we need to have a little talk."

"Uh-oh," Danny breathed.

We went into the other room. Danny sprawled at one end of the sofa and I sat down at the other.

"What is it?" I asked warily.

"We just got a letter from your dad. He's going to a conference in Bismarck next week, and wants to know if you boys want to fly out there when it's over and spend a few days with him. He says it's about a two-hour drive from Bismarck to the North Dakota Badlands. He'll pay for the whole thing, of course."

Danny and I didn't answer.

"There are only three weeks left of vacation," Danny said finally.

"I know. It's completely up to you."

I could tell that Mom was struggling to be neutral. There was no expression in her voice, one way or the other. She could have been reading telephone numbers from a directory.

"What do you think?" I asked her.

"What I think's not important here."

"But what do you think anyway?" I insisted.

"I'm thinking that a couple of days in the Badlands is a poor substitute for two years without seeing you at all. On the other hand, it's a start, and he seems to want to be a part of your lives again, so . . . You *do* need a father."

I wished Danny would decide for me, because part of me wanted to go and part didn't.

But Danny said, "What do you want to do, T.R.?"

"What's in the Badlands?" I asked Mom.

"In the North Dakota Badlands, I'm not sure. The ones in South Dakota are more famous." She shrugged. "Rocks. Gullies. Wildlife." Mom brightened. "It might be a lot of fun. It's really the only vacation you guys will get this summer, I'm afraid."

"Do we have to decide right now?" asked Danny.

"No, but he wants me to call him tomorrow night, so he can get plane tickets for you."

"We'll let you know," Danny said.

I know that Danny must get tired of having to decide everything. When you're the oldest son in the family, you're sort of like the scout, I guess, going out to explore the territory and clear the path for the next to come along, namely me.

It was Danny who was supposed to show me how to be brave at the doctor's, Danny who taught me to tie my shoes, even Danny, along with Mom and Aunt Cis, who taught me to ride a bike. I wonder if Danny ever wonders who's going to be there for him somewhere down the road.

We still hadn't decided by breakfast the next morning, and when we saw the mail truck go by the house, Danny said, "Get the key."

I went into the dining room. The bowl on the table was empty. I went back to Danny. "The key's not there."

"What do you mean?"

"The bowl's empty!"

"I *put* it there! I remember!"

"I looked," I said.

Danny went into the dining room and searched all around. Then he went to Mom. "Do you have the key to Miss Clark's house?"

"Yes," she said.

"We're going to get her mail."

"That's not necessary. She'll be home today. She can get the mail herself and do whatever watering is needed. I'll give it to her when she comes over."

Danny and I looked at each other in horror. I followed him out onto the back steps.

"Danny!" I whispered. "What are we going to *do*?"

"We are cooked!" he moaned. "Baked! Fried!"

"Think we should tell Mom?"

"Are you crazy? What are we going to tell her? That Diane Clark's underwear is under her bed?"

"Maybe we could say that one of the flowerpots was leaking and we want to check before she gets home."

"Mom can smell phony a mile away."

We sat out on the steps hyperventilating. This had to be one of the biggest mistakes we had ever made. I guess we both figured that if we sat there long enough, we could think of some reason to go back to Miss Clark's house, but the next thing we knew, the doorbell rang, and it was Diane Clark herself, asking for her extra key. We could hear her voice all the way out back. "I'm home early," she said. Danny put his head on his arms.

"Boys?" called Mom. "Danny and T.R.! Miss Clark would like to see you."

Danny turned to me. "Let's go to the Badlands," he said. "The sooner the better."

We wished we could be alone with Miss Clark. We sure didn't want Mom to hear what she had to say.

She was standing there in a pink skirt and top, and had a deep tan. She smiled and held out two five-dollar bills. We didn't deserve them, we knew, but we took them anyway.

"Thanks a bunch, guys," she said. "The plants look great. I really appreciate it."

"You're welcome," said Danny.

"Any problem with anything? I forgot to tell you that the kitchen faucet drips, and you have to turn the handle really hard."

"We didn't have any problem with it," I told her.

"Good. Maybe you'll take care of my house again sometime," she said.

"Sure," said Danny.

Mom gave her the key and Miss Clark went back across the street.

"We decided to go to the Badlands," Danny said to Mom.

"Yeah," I said. "The sooner the better."

Mom studied us for a moment. "Okay. I'll call your father."

We both went upstairs and lay facedown on Danny's bed.

"When do you suppose she'll change her underpants?" I asked.

"Tomorrow, probably."

"Think we should go tell her where they are?"

"Are you *nuts*?"

"If we don't, she'll call Mom."

"If we *do*, she'll call Mom."

"Maybe she'll think the maid cleaned out all her drawers and forgot to put the stuff back."

"If she had a maid, T.R., she wouldn't have needed us to water her plants."

"T.R.?" came Mom's voice from below.

I went to the top of the stairs. "Yeah?"

"Come down here a minute. I want to show you something."

I went on down, and Danny came halfway down behind me, just in case, listening from the stairs.

Mom was sitting on the couch with the pile of mail, and she was leafing through a catalog on her lap. "You wanted to see what a garter belt looks like," she said. "There are some in this catalog. Take a good look."

There were two women, a brunette and a blonde. The brunette had on red underwear, the blonde had black. They each wore a bra, bikini panties, and a sort of wide tight-fitting belt that came low over the hips, with long strips of elastic hanging from it attached to the top of nylon stockings.

"So what's the garter?" I said.

"I guess it's that little rubber clip that hooks on to the top of each stocking," Mom said.

But I still didn't get it. "How do they go to the bathroom?" I asked.

Mom laughed. "With difficulty."

Fugitives

Danny and I didn't want to look Miss Clark in the face ever again. Every time the phone rang, we jumped and stared at each other. Another day went by, though, and nothing happened. We thought of every excuse we could to stay inside.

"Maybe she's still wearing clothes from her suitcase," Danny said. "When she runs out of underwear, that's when she'll notice."

But two days later, we still hadn't heard from Miss Clark.

"You guys better think about packing," Mom said. "You'll find clean underwear in that basket on the hamper."

I didn't even want to hear the word "underwear."

"Aunt Cis is going to drive over tonight, then take you to O'Hare tomorrow to catch the plane," Mom said.

I wished we were leaving in five minutes, and that when we got back, we'd find out Miss Clark had moved to Missouri or something. We spent the morning tossing clothes back and forth between our rooms.

"You want this Batman shirt?" Danny asked.

"That's yours. Give me the one with the Joker on it. Uncle Keith gave that one to me," I told him.

When we were done, Mom came upstairs to check our bags. "T.R., this is hardly enough to get you through two days, much less six! You've got to have an extra pair of jeans, at least two good shirts, more socks . . ."

"It's only Dad!" I said. "We're not visiting the President!"

"Clean socks and underwear for every day of the week," Mom insisted.

By one that afternoon, we couldn't pretend to be packing any longer, and knew that Mom would wonder why we were still hanging around the house on our last day home. So after lunch, we went out the back door, grabbed our bikes, and rode over to Paul's.

"Come in!" he called.

He was on the couch in the living room leaning back against a cushion, with Bonkers wrapped around his neck. The cat was purring like crazy, and stretched out his front paws, the claws going out and in with pleasure. In fact, he seemed to be trying to bed down in Paul's hair.

Paul looked like a different person—happier than I'd seen him in a long time.

"Mom used to do this," he said dreamily, reaching up to pet his cat. "When I was sick, I mean. She used to stroke my hair." Then he blushed.

We could tell he was embarrassed to have told us that.

"Mom still strokes our foreheads when we're sick," Danny said. I was glad he said that. I liked knowing that the Desert Rats would cover for each other when someone said something embarrassing. I wished Danny had covered for me when I made that dumb remark to Randall about a garter belt.

"How's Randall's invention working?" I asked.

"Great. Bonkers won't go near the window," Paul said.

I was happy for Bonkers, but a little sad, too. He could never go out on the grass or smell the flowers. What kind of a life was that? A happy one, I guess, the way he looked right then. Maybe I was really worried about Danny and me. We couldn't go out our front door for the rest of our lives without being afraid we'd run into Miss Clark. We were hiding out like we'd just escaped from Stateville.

"I see the sexy babe's back," Paul said, unwrapping Bonkers from around his neck and putting him on his lap. Then he stroked the cat under the chin, and Bonkers looked as though he was hypnotized there on his back, paws limp, his head tipping farther and farther over the edge of Paul's knees. "I saw her car a couple days ago."

"Yeah, she's back," said Danny.

"So does she have sexy underwear or what?" Paul grinned. I just sat there in one of the Bremmers' chairs with my lips pressed together. I wasn't going to answer that question for anything in the world.

But Danny blabbed. "Yeah," he said. "Red and black teddies with lace around the bottoms."

"Yeah?" said Paul. "Yeah? Yeah?"

"Danny!" I mumbled under my breath.

Paul grinned even wider. "You take anything?"

Now I *knew* Paul was going to be the "bad apple" that Aunt Mavis had warned us about. I remembered the time he'd shoplifted a pair of shoelaces at the mall. Or maybe he was just trying to act tough to hide the part of him that was hurting. I'll bet that's what Mom would say.

"Of course we didn't take anything!" said Danny. "What do you think we are?"

"You could have tied something to the handlebars of your bike. You know, the way guys hang stuff from their rearview mirrors."

"Oh, sure!" said Danny. "We go riding down Cajun Drive with a pair of Diane Clark's red underpants waving from the handlebars and she sees us. Then what? We're in trouble enough already."

Uh-oh, I thought.

"What do you mean?" Paul asked.

I elbowed Danny. He realized he'd goofed, and his cheeks were pink.

"Nothing," he said.

Paul grinned. "You *did* take some stuff!"

"We did *not*!" I said. "It's under her bed."

"T.R., you jerk!" yelled Danny, turning to me.

Hoo boy!

"What were you doing under her bed?" asked Paul, and we had to tell him the whole story.

Paul stared. "What are you going to do when she finds her underpants missing?"

"We'll be out of town," Danny said, and told him how

we were going to North Dakota to spend a few days with Dad.

"Well, have fun, you guys," Paul told us, laughing.

We rode up and down Mickey's street until she finally came out on the porch. Norman was already sitting on the steps eating a Popsicle, but Mickey came out with a book and an apple and sat down on the step above him.

Danny and I rode over.

"What'cha reading?" Danny asked her.

She held up the book. *Dinah for President,* it said on the cover. That's Mickey, all right. If she ever ran for anything, it would be number one, you can bet.

"What's up?" she asked.

"We're going to North Dakota for five days to visit Dad," Danny said. "He's got a meeting there or something."

"Yeah?" said Mickey.

"So . . ." Danny shrugged. "I'm just telling you, that's all."

"I'm crying already," said Mickey, and took a bite out of the apple, settling down again with her book.

I don't know what Danny expected her to say, but it wasn't that. He looked embarrassed. We went straight home after that, and decided we wouldn't leave the house again till Aunt Cis came to take us to the airport. When we put our bikes at the side of the house we saw Miss Clark sweeping her sidewalk out front, so we crept around to our back door and went in through the kitchen.

"T.R.," Mom called. "Go get the mail, would you?"

And meet Miss Clark? "I can't," I said. "I think I hurt my ankle."

"Oh, no!" Mom came up from the basement with some jelly jars. "Why do these things happen just before a trip?" She pulled up my pant leg and checked my ankle. "It's not swollen," she said.

"But I don't think I should put any weight on it for a while," I said.

"You were just out riding your bike!"

"Yeah, well, I think I hurt it then."

Danny was already edging past me and starting upstairs.

"Danny?" called Mom.

"I've got to go to the bathroom," he answered.

Mom went back in the kitchen, where she was making preserves from the peaches she'd bought at Hillman's farm.

It was fifteen minutes before Danny tiptoed back down again, and we sat together on the couch reading the comics. I'd glance out the window now and then to see if Miss Clark was still there. She was. She was watering the bushes in her front yard.

Once she stopped to pull up some weeds, and when she bent over, I could see the big blue polka dots of her bikini panties right through her white shorts.

"Danny!" I whispered. "Look!"

He leaned forward and looked past me out the window. "What?"

"Her polka-dot pants! She found them!"

Danny swallowed.

"What if she has *two* pairs and she hasn't looked in her drawer yet?" he said.

"Oh. Right," I said.

Mom poked her head around the corner. "Well? Did we get any mail?"

"Uh . . ." Danny began. "I . . . I don't think it's come yet."

"Did you check?"

"No . . ."

"Will *somebody* please go get the mail?" Mom yelled. "For heaven's sake, do I have to do everything around here?"

"Okay," said Danny. "We'll go."

I knew he was going to make me go with him. Mom watched as we went out the back door. We rode across the grass to the side street, went around the block behind so that we got to the mailboxes on the corner from the other direction, and didn't have to go down Cajun at all.

When we got back, Mom said, "I thought you hurt your ankle, T.R."

"It's better now," I told her. "I just wanted to keep Danny company."

We're a team. We wouldn't have gotten into trouble in the first place if Danny hadn't been trying to teach me about women.

St. Christopher

It's really weird that Aunt Cis is on Dad's side of the family—his sister, in fact. I guess Dad is sort of the skim milk of the Scarlino family, and Aunt Cis is the cream. Aunt Cis and Grandma Flora together, anyway.

She's got black wavy hair like Dad's, with gray just beginning on top. Danny says her eyes are like black olives, but to me they're more like sparklers. You might think she's about to cry because her eyes look wet, but she's not. She laughs. She's always laughing, and after Dad left us—well, after he went off to Greece with his graduate assistant—there wasn't a whole lot to laugh about, but Aunt Cis always found something.

We've driven back to Chicago to visit once since we moved to Rosemary Acres in June, but Aunt Cis hadn't been to see us yet. She's a private duty nurse, and was on a case then.

"I'll wait till you get your curtains up and your pictures hung," she'd said.

So now her yellow car, as bright as the sun, pulled up, and it was loaded down with homemade bread, Aunt Cis's own fettuccini, grapes, apples, a lemon cake, and plum tomatoes from the little garden in her backyard. Danny and I went out to help carry stuff in, and I decided not to worry about Diane Clark. If she came over and asked what happened to her underwear, I'd just hurry Aunt Cis on inside and tell her there was a crazy woman loose at Rosemary Acres.

"Oh, you two, I could squeeze you to death!" Aunt Cis cried, swooping us both toward her so that our heads bumped. And then she stood facing our town house with its gray shutters and blue door, like all the other town houses in the development, and gave a pleased sigh. "So this is Rosemary Acres," she said. "It's lovely."

Two months ago, Danny and I would have gagged at the word "lovely," but now that we'd met Mickey and Paul and Randall—now that we'd had some adventures, stuff to talk about—it didn't seem all that bad.

Mom came out and Aunt Cis let go of us, wrapping her arms around Mom instead. "Oh, Kath," she said, "it's beautiful!" (Mom's name is Kathleen, but since Dad left and she and Aunt Cis got really close, Cis calls her "Kath.")

When we got inside and Aunt Cis had seen all our rooms, I heard her say to Mom, "I'm really amazed you could find something affordable so close to Chicago. So much space!" And Mom said, "Well, Tom was very generous. I'll say that for him."

We ate dinner then. Mom had fixed a roast chicken,

but everything else was from Aunt Cis. It was almost like being back in her house again, with all the wonderful cooking smells—both from her kitchen and the houses next door—and I wondered for the tenth time why nobody had ever fallen in love with Aunt Cis and married her. I figure you could love her for her lemon cake alone!

As soon as she'd finished eating, Aunt Cis pushed her coffee cup away, looked right at Danny, and said, "So when do I get to meet this Mickey I've been hearing so much about?"

Danny looked at her, then glared at me.

"Not me," I said.

"Flora," Aunt Cis explained. "She tells me everything."

"Mickey's just a friend," said Danny.

"Okay. I'll buy that," said Aunt Cis.

"One of the Desert Rats," I explained.

"Desert?" asked Aunt Cis.

"No trees," said Danny. "No big ones, anyway."

"Unless you go down to Lake Tarragon or over to Hill-man's farm," I explained.

"Well, if this is a desert, it's a pretty nice one. You guys lucked out," said Aunt Cis.

The doorbell rang and I answered. It was Randall.

"Hey, Mickey said you were going away for a week," he said.

"Yeah. We're going to visit my dad," I told him.

He handed me a folded piece of notebook paper, taped around something that felt like a fifty-cent piece. "Well, she asked me to give you this. I saw her at the pool."

I turned it over in my hand. "Give it to *me*?"

Randall raised his shoulders so that the skier on the front of his *Ski New Hampshire* T-shirt seemed to straighten a little, then let them down and the skier crouched again. "She just said 'Give it to those guys,' that's all."

"Okay. You want some lemon cake, Randall? Aunt Cis is here."

"I never say no to cake," said Randall, and followed me out to the kitchen. By the time I'd said, "Aunt Cis, this is my friend Randall," Mom was already reaching for a saucer and cut him a big hunk of cake.

"Hi, Randall," said Aunt Cis. "You're the genius I've been hearing about, huh?"

Randall gave a shy smile.

"You ever come to Chicago?" she asked.

"Only to the museums and stuff," Randall said. "Too many gangs and rough stuff, Dad says."

"Well, there's aren't any gangs in my neighborhood, Randall. Just a lot of nice Italian families. The next time T.R. comes to see me, you come, too, and I'll treat you both to the best *gelato* (that's Italian for ice cream) in the state of Illinois."

"I could stand that," said Randall, and dug into her lemon cake.

I slipped Danny the paper from Mickey when I thought no one was looking, but Aunt Cis saw it out of the corner of her eye.

"What's this?" asked Danny.

"Something from Mickey. She gave it to Randall at the pool and asked him to give it to us."

"Just a friend, huh?" Aunt Cis teased, grinning at Danny.

Danny tipped back in his chair so Aunt Cis and Mom couldn't read the paper, and pulled off the tape. There was something round and bronze-colored that looked like a coin. Danny let me read the note, since it was for me, too:

> I didn't mean to sound rude yesterday, you guys. I guess I just didn't want to say anything in front of Norman. Anyway, this place is going to be deadly till you get back. Here's something to keep in your pocket, Danny.
>
> Mickey

Danny was really blushing then.

"Why, it's a St. Christopher medal," said Aunt Cis, reaching over for the round shiny thing. "You know what that's for, don't you, Danny?"

"How should I know? We're not Catholic," Danny said.

"We're religious ignoramuses," I added, quoting Grandma Flora.

Aunt Cis laughed. "I think it's a very thoughtful gift. St. Christopher is the patron saint of travelers. It's a way of wishing you a safe trip."

"Oh," said Danny, and wrapped it back up in Mickey's note. I know Mickey's his age, not mine, and I was glad she'd included me in the note, but couldn't she have found something for me to put in *my* pocket? I'd even settle for the prize in a Cracker Jack box, as long as it came from Mickey.

After Randall left, Danny went upstairs and I followed. He went into his room and started to close the door, but I was there in the doorway.

"What do you want?" he asked.

"Just wondered what you were going to do with that St. Christopher medal."

"I don't know."

"Looks as if she really likes you."

"The note was for both of us, T.R."

"Yeah, but the St. Christopher thing was for you."

He just shrugged.

"If you don't want it, Danny, could I keep it in *my* pocket?" I asked.

"No," said Danny, and shut the door.

The Sears Tower Hamburger

The worst part about driving away from Rosemary Acres with Aunt Cis was leaving Mom. The best part was knowing that we wouldn't run into Miss Clark for the next six days.

I wondered if she'd forget about her underwear in six days. Or—and this thought didn't come to me till we were out on the freeway—maybe she'd go over and talk to Mom while we were gone and tell her what happened.

For a moment, I felt panicky in my chest. Like what if our plane went down and Mom never saw us again and the last thing she'd hear about us was that we had looked through a woman's dresser drawers. What if Miss Clark showed up at our funeral and said, "They were good kids, even though they did snoop through my underwear."

I wanted to grab the door handle and yell, "Stop the car! I'm getting out!" But then I figured if that ever happened—our funeral, I mean—Mom would figure it had been Danny's idea, since he's the oldest, and she'd blame it on him. So it was really Danny's worry, not mine. Besides, Aunt Cis said there might be time to get a sundae before we got on the plane; I put my mind on that.

Danny was sitting up front with Aunt Cis, and I had the backseat to myself. I liked looking at Aunt Cis's hair, the way the sun came through the window and made the gray on top of her head all silver, like she had metallic threads woven in her hair.

For a while Aunt Cis had been all bubbly and fun after we left Rosemary Acres. She and Danny were trading jokes, and as soon as Danny told one, Aunt Cis had another ready. We'd had a good time the night before, too. We all played Clue at the dining-room table, and Aunt Cis and I each won a game. But suddenly I realized how quiet it was inside the car, and then Aunt Cis said, "I'd just like to say something to you guys before you see your dad." She cleared her throat a little. "I know it's hard to forgive him for leaving the family, but in spite of everything, he really does love you."

If he really loved us, I was thinking, how come it was Aunt Cis telling us, not him?

"I'm not asking you to forgive him. And I know you can't *forget* even if you wanted to, because it's hurt you and your mom a lot. But remember that nobody really knows what goes on in a marriage except the two people in it, and sometimes even they're confused."

I concentrated on Aunt Cis's eyes in the rearview mirror. She wasn't looking at me, though, or even Danny—she was staring straight ahead.

"All we can do is accept that they're divorced now, and not waste too much time trying to figure out the 'whys' or 'if onlys.' That can drive you nuts. So what I'm asking is that you give Tom a chance. You guys need a father and he's at least trying. He may never be the kind of dad you really want or need, but let him be a dad in his own way, and maybe, as you get older, you'll understand him better. That's all I'm saying."

Danny didn't move. "Okay," he said, without expression.

"Sure," I told her.

"I'm *really* glad you're meeting him in North Dakota. I mean, I'm sure it cost a lot of money to buy your plane tickets on such short notice, but . . ."

"He got them free, on his frequent flyer miles," said Danny.

"Oh," said Aunt Cis, and tapped her finger against the steering wheel. "Well, I know you're going to have a great time in the Badlands. I've never been there. Maybe someday . . ."

We finally found a parking space at O'Hare and, just as Aunt Cis said, there was time for caramel sundaes before we boarded the plane.

Man, I hate planes! I've only been on them a few times, but I hated them all. First you have to go down this narrow aisle with your carry-on bag, and you always manage to bump into a businessman who gives you this look, and then you get to your seat and find out your overhead luggage compartment is already filled, so you have to put your stuff in a compartment way at the back, which means that when the plane lands and everyone comes charging down the aisle, you've got to wait till they all leave before you can go back and get your things, so you're always the last one off.

I usually have to go to the bathroom, too, about the time the seat belt light comes on, and when I finally get a chance to go, the flight attendant comes along with a cart and tells me to sit back down. Mom took us to Florida once to visit Grandma Flora, and the flight was so bumpy that the seat belt light stayed on the whole time and I didn't get to the bathroom at all. Not to mention that there's hardly any room to put your feet, and the food tastes like tennis shoes.

This time, though, it was a short flight from Chicago to Minneapolis, and then Minneapolis to Bismarck. About the time I'd finished my Coke and peanuts, the pilot was telling us what the weather in Bismarck would be like and the seat belt light had come on again.

Like I said, we were the last ones off the plane. Dad was pacing back and forth in the waiting room with his arms folded over his chest. I saw him look at his watch just before he caught sight of us, and then he smiled and waved.

"I *wondered* where you guys were," he said, slapping us both on the shoulders. "Here, let me help carry those. Boy, you sure travel light. Hope you've got some good hiking boots in there. Got a windbreaker? Lots of socks?"

"Yeah, Mom made us bring a lot of everything," I said as we headed for the exit.

"Good for her," said Dad.

* * *

The first evening with Dad went pretty well. He got a motel with a pool, so before dinner Danny and I whooped it up while Dad sat in a deck chair talking with a woman who had a little girl. The kid was in the wading pool wearing an inflatable ring around her waist and water wings that made her arms look like Popeye's.

We'd probably been horsing around in the pool for over an hour when Dad finally called, "You fellas hungry yet? I'm starved. What do you say we get some dinner?"

I wanted to stay in another ten minutes, but Danny thought we probably should go, so we got out and dressed and Dad took us to this restaurant he said was the best in town because he was hungry for a really good steak. I was hungry for a burger, but there weren't any on the menu.

"Only at lunch," the waiter said.

"Filet mignon, now that would be good," Dad said, looking over the selections. "The veal, too."

I was looking at Dad, though, wondering what he looked like when he lived with us. I think maybe his face was a little fuller now. There was some gray in his hair, but not as much as Aunt Cis had in hers.

"I guess I'll try the fried chicken," said Danny.

The more I studied the menu, the more I wanted a hamburger. The waiter stood over me with his pencil ready.

"I really wanted a hamburger," I said.

"They don't *have* hamburgers, T.R.," Dad said. "Only at lunch. Choose something else."

I just couldn't see ordering veal for fifteen bucks and not eating it. "Maybe just some french fries then," I said. Dad frowned. I guess they didn't serve fries at dinner either.

Then the waiter said, "We have a different kitchen crew for lunch and dinner. But if the boy wants a hamburger, I'll check with our dinner chef and see what he can do." He took Dad's order and left.

Dad propped his elbows on the table, his chin touching his fingertips. "Sometimes," he said, "we need to be a little adventurous. Try something new. Believe it or not, there was probably a time you didn't like pizza, either, T.R., but you learned."

I just sat there putting my fork on my knife, then my spoon on the fork, then taking the knife out from under the bottom and putting it on the spoon, till at last the pile fell over and I had to pick the fork up off the floor.

Danny gave me a nudge, and the next time I looked across the table at Dad he was sort of staring off into the space above my head. I remembered what Aunt Cis had said about giving him a chance, so I sat back in my seat and folded my hands in my lap. Dad smiled.

"I wonder why you can have hamburgers for lunch but not for dinner," I said, just to break the silence.

"It helps limit the number of different things the chef has to cook," Dad explained.

"But if the stuff's right there, couldn't he fry a hamburger as fast as a steak?"

"Sure, but there have to be some kind of rules, T.R., that's what makes the world go round."

I sat there thinking about the rules back at Rosemary Acres, which ones made sense and which ones seemed stupid. "Some rules are really dumb," I said.

"I agree," Dad went on. "And when enough people decide that a rule or law is stupid, they usually do something about it and get it changed. What you need to ask yourself, whenever you think a rule is useless and that it wouldn't hurt if you broke it, is what would happen if everyone broke it."

"But is a hamburger really such a big deal?"

"On the face of things, no. But if everyone in this dining room asked for something that wasn't on the dinner menu, there would be chaos in the kitchen. The chef is bending the rules tonight for you."

I looked across at Danny and wondered if he was thinking about Paul and his cat, same as me. If everybody at Rosemary Acres was allowed to have a cat, would that be so awful? And if cats were allowed, then I suppose dogs would have to be allowed, too. I just couldn't see the harm in it. A lot of poop to watch out for, but I could live with that.

Danny *was* thinking about Paul Bremmer. "What if," he said, "it wouldn't be a good idea if everybody did something, but for one certain person, it was about the only right thing to do?"

"Then that would be a special case, and there are exceptions, of course, to every rule," said Dad.

The hamburger arrived with the steak and chicken, and it was the weirdest thing I ever saw. It was as wide as a pancake but about four times as thick, and it teetered on a hunk of French bread, with another hunk on top. I mean, you'd have to be Godzilla to get something like that in your mouth.

"We couldn't seem to find the buns," the waiter said.

There were toothpicks with little cellophane feathers on them holding the mess together, a cherry tomato on one of the toothpicks and an olive on the other. All I could do was stare.

"Thank you very much," Dad said to the waiter. "I'm sure it will be delicious."

What I was sure of was that they should have sent their chef to McDonald's for lessons.

Danny and I looked at each other and started to laugh. Then we were all laughing, Dad included.

"The Sears Tower Hamburger," said Dad, referring to one of the tallest buildings in the world, which just happens to be in Chicago.

I thought I'd break my jaws, though, trying to get my teeth around the stupid thing. I made several passes at it for practice, snapping my jaws like an alligator.

"Take it apart, T.R., and use only half the bread," Dad said.

I ate a couple bites and quit. It was probably the worst hamburger I ever had in my life—too soft and too wet, not flat and salty like the ones at McDonald's—and I'll bet it set Dad back ten bucks. But maybe it was worth it just to see him laugh. Maybe Aunt Cis was right, and we'd get to be buddies after all.

World's Largest Holstein Cow

This is going to be an adventure!" Dad said the next morning as we headed for the Badlands. I liked the sound of it. Would anybody ever go to a place called the Goodlands?

I sat in the front seat this time and Danny sprawled out in back as though he was glad he could have the seat all to himself. Then I wished I'd sat in back with him.

"It'll be nice doing something together—a guy kind of thing," Dad said, looking at me and winking. "I'm figuring on one day there, one day exploring the park, and one day back, with time to stop and see things on the way."

We hadn't gone more than thirty miles, though, when I had to go to the bathroom.

"I have to go to the bathroom, Dad," I said.

"Already? Ye gods, T.R., we just started out. You should have thought of that before we left."

"Tell that to my intestines," I said, and heard Danny

laugh in the backseat. I like it when I can make Danny laugh.

"Okay. I'll look for a gas station," Dad said.

I could feel the car slow down every time something came into view that could have been a gas station. At last Dad pulled over to this crummy place that didn't even look as though it was open. The door to the men's room, in fact, was off its hinges.

I got out of the car and went over. It hadn't been cleaned in a million years. You'd have to be decontaminated if you even sat down on the seat. I went back out.

"There isn't any toilet paper," I said.

Danny was trying not to laugh. I almost laughed, too.

Dad sighed, "T.R., can't you just make do?"

"There aren't any paper towels, either. There isn't even any water!"

"Get in," said Dad.

So we went another ten miles and found an Amoco station. When I got in the car again, I decided to sit in back with Danny.

Dad said, "Next time, come prepared." Somehow that set us off.

"Yeah," Danny said. "Always carry a roll of toilet paper in your pocket, T.R." I laughed so hard I was afraid I might have to go to the bathroom again.

Dad didn't say anything for a while, and Danny and I concentrated on the scenery. In every direction we looked we could see way off in the distance. There were small peaked hills on the horizon.

Danny pointed out a huge farm machine of some kind

perched on a slope. It looked like a monster insect ready to come down and devour a sleeping village.

"The Great Grasshopper from Mars," Danny said, and this time Dad laughed.

We were somewhere between Bismarck and Dickinson when we began to see signs advertising "The World's Largest Holstein Cow."

"Hey, Dad! Can we stop?" I asked. I tried to imagine the largest cow in the world.

"We'll see," said Dad.

"How big do you suppose it is?" I went on. "Three tons?"

"Probably takes six men to milk her," Danny said.

"Hooves the size of buckets," said Dad, getting into the act.

"And think of the cow patties!" I said, and this time we all laughed.

I told Dad about the Rosemary Acres picnic right after we'd moved in, and how everyone had played cow pattie bingo over on Hillman's farm.

"Played *what*?" asked Dad.

"The farmer marked the pasture off into squares, and each square had a number. Everyone picked a number, and then the farmer let a cow out. If the cow pooped in your square, you won," I explained.

"You're kidding," said Dad. "You guys are out in farm country now, aren't you?"

"It's okay," said Danny.

"Yeah, I like it there," I said. If it wasn't for what you did, I was thinking, looking at the back of Dad's neck, we'd still be living in Chicago near Aunt Cis, and you'd be teaching at the University, and you and Mom would still be married. Dad's got an ugly neck.

"World's Largest Holstein Cow," read another sign. "Golden West Shopping Center, Five Miles."

"Please stop there, Dad. I really want to see that cow," I said.

As it turned out, we didn't have to stop at all. The World's Largest Holstein Cow was a huge statue up on a hill.

"What a rip-off!" said Danny.

"That's no fair," I protested.

But this time it was Dad who thought it was funny. "Well, they didn't say 'World's Largest Live Cow,' now, did they?" Dad's got a weird sense of humor.

The closer we got to the Badlands, the stranger the land became. Big cracks in the ground. Gullies and layers of colored rock along the sides.

"Wow!" I said, hanging out the window.

"Awesome!" Danny said.

It was like being on the moon.

In the Theodore Roosevelt National Park, we got a trail map with names like Buckhorn Trail and Wind Canyon, Slump Block Pullout, and Cannonball Concretions Pullout. As we followed the winding road, we saw a herd of buffalo far out in a field and at least two porcupines waddling along the side of the road. Dad let us get out and then he tried to take a picture of one, but it scurried into the scrub brush and spread out its quills so that its backside looked like part of the bush.

Dad parked finally and we took the Lone Tree Loop Trail. The brochure said that rattlesnakes sometimes attacked without warning, and that black widow spiders often lived in prairie dog burrows. We didn't see any rattlesnakes, though, and I looked in about a dozen burrows and didn't see any spiders either.

Dad's a pretty good hiker. While we were hiking he said he keeps in shape by jogging ten miles on weekends and working out on a rowing machine three times a week.

"You live in a house or what?" Danny asked. It seemed really weird to be asking our own dad these questions, but when your father drops back into your life after two years, there's a lot you don't know. Probably a lot you don't even want to know.

"A small apartment," Dad said. "There's an exercise room in the basement, though."

We tramped on farther.

"You live alone?" I asked finally.

"T.R.!" Danny warned under his breath.

But Dad said, "Yes. I do now. . . ." And then, "The reason I haven't asked you guys to visit me in Berkeley is that I don't have any place for you to sleep. I've only got one bedroom, and the couch isn't a sleep sofa."

"We could always bring our sleeping bags," I said. Danny kicked my foot and gave me a pained look, meaning he didn't want to go visit Dad at all. I'm not sure I did either. I don't even know why I said it.

"That's an idea!" said Dad, but he didn't say any more than that.

He sure did take a lot of pictures. He was already pointing out lignite and bentonite, and though some of it was interesting, I began to wish he'd shut up and let us look at what we wanted. I didn't understand why we couldn't just enjoy the whole scene, the big sky, and to heck with the names of rocks.

But then I guess it's hard for a man who teaches at a university to understand what guys our age like. I asked Mom once what kind of work he did, and she said he was a paleobotanist.

"Now what do we have here, T.R.?" he asked, pointing to a plant.

I shrugged and stared at the plant. "A weed?"

"You weren't paying attention back there, were you?" Dad said. I guess he was disappointed in me.

The thing was, we only had these couple days in the Badlands, and I still hadn't seen a coyote or anything. Danny and I liked to leap over some of the smaller cracks and gullies, and to Dad that must have seemed a waste.

"Hey, boys!" he said finally, when Danny and I were racing along trying to keep up with a jackrabbit. "You can chase rabbits anytime, but how often do you get to see rocks like this?"

We quit jumping around then and followed Dad, listening to him tell about which layers of rock dated back to prehistoric times. The thing is, the whole *earth* is prehistoric! I mean, the whole shebang was here before man, so why get excited about one little layer? I don't get it.

By the time we made the loop and got back to where we'd parked, Danny and I had botany and geology coming out of our ears.

"Darn!" said Dad, checking his camera. "I've only got two more shots left on this roll. I thought I had more film in my pocket."

"Could I take the last two pictures?" I begged. I was bored out of my skull. "*Please*, Dad?"

Dad looked doubtful.

"This is a very unusual area, T.R. You should think carefully about what you want to remember for the rest of your life. Yes, I guess you and Danny can take the last two shots. You take one and let Danny take the other. Surprise me."

Then he gave us a three-minute demonstration on how to work the camera, how to focus and check the exposure. It would be just my luck to drop it, I thought.

Dad looked around and saw some other hikers coming along the trail. "Tell you what, boys, I've got to take a leak." He grinned. "I'm going behind a bush or something. Stay right there."

He went up the trail and stepped behind a bank of rocks.

I held Dad's camera in my hands and waited till the other hikers had gone by. Then I looked around at the hills and ravines and stuff. I held the camera up to my eye and tried to think what I wanted to remember about our trip to the North Dakota Badlands. I guess the most important thing was that Danny and I were here together.

"Open your mouth." I grinned.

Danny looked at me and started to smile. He opened his mouth as wide as he could.

Click.

I got his tonsils and we laughed. I turned the film forward and handed the camera to him.

"Open your mouth," he said.

Click.

He got mine.

Of Babies and Belly Buttons

We spent the next day hiking, and because it was our last full day in the park, we stayed right up to closing time. Dad found this motel where we could spend the night, and said we had to take showers before we ate dinner, because we were sweating like pigs. He says when you get to be Danny's age you develop a "stag odor," which is probably right, because Danny's armpits smell different from mine already.

We were pretty tired. We'd hiked every trail we could, but that's the way Dad is: thorough. All through dinner it was as though he was trying to make up for the two years he hadn't been around to teach us anything: that real scoria comes from volcanoes; that it was Teddy Roosevelt who established national parks; that you could see cactus in the Badlands, and the meadowlark was the state bird. The way to make points with my father, I guessed, was to always have an interesting fact on the tip of your tongue.

Finally, when he stopped for breath and reached for the catsup, I remembered an interesting fact of my own.

"Hey, Dad," I said, "do you know what they do in the Arctic to keep their hands from freezing?"

Dad focused his attention on me. "No," he said. "I don't."

"I heard it from one of the guys in school last year. His uncle was sent to Antarctica on a scientific expedition, and whenever a man went outdoors, he had to have a partner. You know why?"

Dad shook his head. Danny began to smile because he already knew the answer.

"So that if one guy made the mistake of touching something metal with his bare hand and the skin froze to the metal, the other guy could pee on it and unfreeze it," I announced.

Dad slowly set the catsup bottle back on the table and looked at me incredulously.

"It's *true*, Dad! That's what they were told to do!"

"I think it's pretty smart," said Danny. "It's like you said, Dad. Be prepared." He laughed then, and so did Dad. "Of course," Danny went on, "if the guy touches something overhead and the skin freezes, it's going to be sort of hard for his partner."

We all laughed some more.

"I wonder how cold it has to get in Antarctica before your pee freezes as soon as it comes out," I said.

Danny was cracking up. "Imagine having to go around with an icicle on the end of your . . ."

"Okay, okay," Dad laughed. "Let's eat."

Dinner helped, and when it was time for dessert, we each ordered a brownie sundae with whipped cream and cherries sliding down a river of hot fudge sauce.

Back in our room, Dad took one of the double beds and Danny and I took the other. We lay there in the dark talking about what we'd liked most about the Badlands, and after a while Dad said, "It's been fun. We need more times like this, don't we?"

"Yeah," I said.

"Yeah," said Danny.

"You're growing up fast, and I just wondered if there's anything you guys need to know about." He paused. "Maybe there are things you feel you can't ask your mother."

What was this? I wondered. The old birds-and-bees talk? Danny nudged me with his elbow. Actually, Mom had done a pretty good job of it. She'd explained about sex and stuff. It was embarrassing, all right, but we got the answers we needed.

Danny, though, decided to play dumb. "Yeah, I was sort of wondering if . . . uh . . ."

"Yes?" came Dad's voice from the other bed.

"Well," Danny went on, "a girl can't get pregnant if she has sex standing up, can she?"

I pulled the sheet up over my mouth to keep from laughing out loud and could feel the bed shaking as Danny went into a fit of silent giggling.

"Is *that* old story still making the rounds?" Dad said. "That's absolutely false, guys. It doesn't matter *how* a couple have sex, if they don't use a contraceptive, the woman could be standing on her head and she still might get pregnant. In fact, not even contraceptives are one-hundred percent safe."

"You can have sex standing on your head?" I asked, and Danny and I had to keep poking each other under the covers to keep quiet.

Dad must have known we were giggling, but he probably figured we were just embarrassed. When he answered, we could tell he was smiling, too. "Well, I've never tried it, but I suppose it could be done."

Danny, though, was on a roll, so he kept going: "But a girl can't get pregnant till she's eighteen, can she?"

Dad gasped, and Danny and I dived under the covers again and stuffed our fists in our mouths because we were laughing so hard.

"Good grief! Where do you guys pick up this stuff? Once a girl starts having her monthly periods, she can get pregnant if she's sexually active. In fact, she can get pregnant the very first time she has sex. Girls as young as eleven and twelve have been known to become mothers. I hope I've made *that* clear." And then he added, "I'm really surprised that you boys know so little. I've *told* Kathleen that if there's anything she can't handle, she can call me. So can you."

We stopped laughing then. I think we were both sorry that our joke turned out to be a joke on Mom. We hadn't meant it that way.

"Mom's doing all right," said Danny, defending her.

"Well, of course she is. You've got a great mom," said Dad.

"Then why did you leave her?" I asked before I could stop myself.

Now the room was really quiet.

"Because I . . . because, for a time, I fell in love with someone else. That's over, but I guess both Kathleen and I are happier apart. It's as simple as that."

It might have been simple to Dad, but it wasn't to us.

"Are you ever going to get back together?" asked Danny.

"Well, 'ever' is a long time. I don't think so. And I don't think Kath would take me back even if I wanted to come."

It was right then, I guess, I wished I hadn't come to the Badlands, because I didn't want to hear what Dad just said. Even though down deep I figured that's probably the way it was between him and Mom, I wanted to hope that maybe someday they'd change and decide they really missed each other.

"Well," said Dad finally, "guess it's time we got some sleep. We've got to get up at seven if we're going to get back to Bismarck and make our planes. Good night, guys."

"'Night, Dad," said Danny.

"Good night," I said.

I don't know when the others fell asleep, but it took me a long time. I sort of forgot about the rocks and gullies and buffalo and porcupine after that. The Badlands, for me, will always be bad. Bad news.

On the way to the airport the next day, Dad kept the radio tuned to NPR, which is a lot of people talking,

talking, talking. I was glad Danny was up front this time, because I had the backseat to myself and slept most of the way.

"Well," Dad said at the gate just before Danny and I boarded, "my flight isn't for another hour yet, so I guess I'll go get some coffee. We're going to do things like this again. It was fun, wasn't it?"

"Sure," said Danny. "Thanks for everything, Dad."

"Yeah, thanks, Dad," I said. I couldn't resist: "Thanks for explaining about rocks and sex and stuff."

Danny tried to stop a chuckle from coming up his throat and it came out his nose instead. That made *me* start laughing.

Dad smiled tolerantly and gave us each a hug. "Well, have a good trip back, now."

We handed the attendant our passes and walked down the ramp to the plane with our carry-on bags bumping against our legs. I turned once to wave to Dad one last time, but he'd already gone.

Moment of Truth

Mom met us at O'Hare, and I hoped she wouldn't ask if Dad had said he wanted to come back. She didn't.

"I *missed* you guys!" she said on the way home.

"We missed you, too," I told her. It was the truth.

Danny told her about the Badlands and the buffalo and porcupines, and I told her about the World's Largest Holstein Cow, because I liked to see her laugh.

"So you had a good time!" she said, as though adding "The End" to the adventure.

"Yeah," I said, "but I'm glad we're home." I couldn't wait to see all the Rats, and called Randall.

"Heeey! Tin Roof, you're back!" he said. "Guess what I've got for Paul's cat."

"Can't imagine," I told him.

"It only works in the bathroom, though," he said. "You attach this cord to the faucet, see, stretch it across the bathroom window, the cat leaps up on the window ledge, and the shower comes on. Cats hate water."

"The windows in the bathrooms are all frosted glass, Randall. Nobody would see Bonkers if he jumped up there anyway," I told him. Sometimes Randall *isn't* such a genius.

"Oh, shoot!" he said. "Well, you'd need a fifty-pound cat, anyway."

Danny called Paul next, but nobody was home. "Probably at the pool," Danny said.

"So's Mickey, I'll bet!" I told him. I knew he wanted to see Mickey even more than he wanted to see Paul, especially after that note she wrote us. "Why don't you call her?"

"No way," said Danny.

"Why not?"

"She might hang up on me."

"Why would she do that?"

"'Cause I'd probably say something stupid."

It always surprises me when Danny chickens out. To me, he looks great, and he's smart, the kind of guy any girl would fall for. One of the things I'm learning from Danny—that he doesn't even know he's teaching me—is that you can look as though you have everything, and still feel shaky inside. The way Paul feels, I guess. Getting his mom's cat back, I think, was about the best thing that ever happened to him.

We put our stuff away and asked Mom if she wanted to come to the pool with us.

"I'm making dinner," she said. "I'll pass. You guys go have fun."

We pulled denim shorts over our bathing trunks,

picked up our towels, and headed for the pool. I think
we were almost as eager to see the gang as we were to
see Mom. They were like family.

Mickey was there, all right, with both her
brothers–Norm, her stepbrother, and little Gus, her half
brother.

"Hi, Danny!" She smiled when she saw us. I was ready
to feel left out, but she added, "Hi, T.R. Have a good
time?"

"Sort of," I said.

Mickey was sitting on the edge of the wading pool with
her freckled legs wrapped around Gus to hold him up.
Boy, she must have a thousand freckles on her legs and
arms.

Gus was slapping at the water with both hands, then
looking startled when it splashed in his face. He was
drooling, too, and every so often a large string of spit
dropped down into the water.

I'll bet the bacteria count in the wading pool is really
something. How many babies, do you suppose, pee in the
pool? All of them. It's really gross.

"How you doin'?" Danny said, and sat down beside
Mickey.

Man, he was smooth when he did that! *How you doin'*?
Just like a twenty-year-old man. His leg was almost touching hers, too. I leaned over to check. It *was* touching!

I wanted to tell Mickey about the World's Largest Hol-
stein Cow, but that was Danny's opener. "Hey," he said.
"Have you ever seen the World's Largest Holstein Cow?"
I mean, I was *saving* that line!

I sat down on the other side of Mickey, but I couldn't sit close to her because Norman had left his stupid mask and snorkel there. I figured she'd notice if I moved his stuff out of the way, even though she and Danny were busy talking.

Norm the Nerd was walking across the wading pool toward us on his hands. He looked like a seal with flippers, his legs trailing out behind him in the water. I don't know how Mickey can stand him.

He *was* pretending to be a seal.

"I'm a seal," he said, and sort of oozed up the side of the wading pool and sat down next to me. He was more like a slug. At least I could try my line on Norman.

"Have you ever seen the World's Largest Holstein Cow?" I asked him.

"Sure," said Norman.

I blinked. "Where?"

"On my granddad's farm. He's got this *really* big cow. It's so big it's a bull."

"That's not it, Norman! I mean a giant-size cow!"

"Nope," said Norman.

"Well, I have. And you know what it was?"

"Nope."

"A statue. A stupid statue of a cow up on a hillside," I told him.

"So what's the good of that?" he said, and slipped back into the water, handwalking across the bottom to the other side and barking like a seal. If he was my brother, I'd push him under.

Mickey and Danny were ignoring me totally, so I

finally got up and went over to the big pool. I did a can-nonball at the deep end, and then I went up on the div-ing board and practiced my somersault dive. I still couldn't do it, but I came close. I swam around for about ten minutes, waiting for Danny to come in, or Paul, or Randall, but nobody showed. Finally I got out, dried off, and stretched out on a deck chair.

The vinyl slats were warm, and I guess I was still sleepy from having to get up so early that morning. As I lay there, I could feel my eyes beginning to close. My legs and arms grew heavy, and I drifted off. Every so often a sudden splash or the lifeguard's whistle woke me for a moment, but then my eyes would close again. It felt good.

I don't know how long I was there, but the next time I opened my eyes halfway, I saw Diane Clark, in her silver and black bathing suit, wiping her back with a towel and looking straight at me. Then, like a nightmare come true, she sat down on the deck chair next to me and stretched out her legs.

I swallowed. I couldn't get up and go dive in the pool, it would be too obvious. I closed my eyes again and pre-tended I was asleep.

It's working! I thought. Maybe she didn't even recog-nize me.

"T.R.?" she said.

Oh, no! I kept my breathing regular, my chest moving slowly up and down.

"Hey! Anybody home?" she said, and only a dead man couldn't hear that.

My eyes opened, but I didn't dare look at her. I stared straight ahead.

"T.R.," she said again. "What went on in my bedroom?"

How could this be happening? It wasn't fair! Why didn't she ask Danny and me together, so we could at least take turns answering? I opened my mouth, but my lips were so dry they stuck together.

"We were looking for a garter belt," I mumbled.

She swung her legs around and leaned forward. "*What?*"

I had to say it again. I still couldn't look at her. I lay with my feet pointing out in opposite directions, a real dork.

"We were looking for a garter belt," I explained. "I'm really sorry!"

She didn't say anything for a moment, but I could feel her eyes staring right through me. "A *garter* belt? What were you going to *do* with it?"

Oh, brother!

"I just . . . some of the guys at school . . ." My voice squeaked like Mickey Mouse and my face burned. "Well, I've heard them talk about it . . . I just wanted to see . . . Danny said . . . I mean, Paul thought . . ."

"So you and Danny went through my drawers to see if I had one," she said. "How many other guys were up there?"

"None. Just me and Danny."

"How did my pants get under the bed?"

Why couldn't there be a tidal wave right then? I wondered. Why couldn't a small earthquake take place in the state of Illinois, just enough to cause a big wave to roll over the surface of the pool and wash me overboard?

"Mom walked in," I said.

"Oh." She got the point. "You and Danny were looking through my drawers when your mom came over, and you stuffed the evidence under the bed."

"Something like that," I said miserably. "We planned to put everything back the next day, but Mom wouldn't give us the key."

"Smart lady," said Diane. She was quiet again, and her quiet was almost worse than her questions.

"Well, I was young once and I understand," she said at last, "but I do have to say that I'm disappointed in you guys. It's sort of creepy to come home and find that somebody's been going through your personal stuff."

"I know we shouldn't have done it," I bleated.

"Did you take anything? To show your friends?"

"No!" I glanced over at her, horrified, then quickly focused on the lifeguard again. "Of course not! We weren't planning to *steal* anything!"

"I see."

"We'll give you your ten dollars back if you want," I offered.

Diane Clark thought about it a minute. "No, but I need your promise that the next time you take care of my house, I can trust you not to go through my things."

Now I *did* stare at her. "You'd ask us again?"

She smiled. "I believe in second chances. If you goof off again, though, I tell your mom everything. Otherwise, she'll never know."

"Thanks!" I said gratefully. "Thanks a lot!"

I sat up and was about to go tell Danny when I saw Paul standing over by the fence with a pillowcase slung over his shoulder. He motioned to me.

"Excuse me," I told Miss Clark.

I picked up my towel and went around the deep end, over to the fence where Paul was standing.

"When did you get back?" he asked.

"An hour ago. Danny called you, but no one answered." I stared at the pillowcase. It looked like a hobo's sack. "What are you doing, running away?"

"*Meow*," said the pillowcase.

Smuggling Bonkers

What's going on?" I asked.

"You've got to help me hide Bonkers," Paul said. "I got a call from maintenance. A man's coming by to inspect our electrical outlets; some of them are defective. The office wants to check out all the ones on our block."

This was it! Another job for the Rats.

"Today or tomorrow. It could be anytime, and Dad won't be home until late."

"*Meow*," came Bonkers again.

"*Shhh*," said Paul, cradling the pillowcase in his arms.

"Can't you just lock him in the bathroom?" I asked.

"There are electrical outlets in the bathroom."

"What about a closet?"

"You can't put Bonkers in a closet. He'd yowl," said Paul. "They'd hear him." He turned and looked around the pool. "Go get Danny," he said.

We ought to have a secret signal, I thought, as I walked along the fence toward the wading pool. I tried to get Danny's attention. Since he and Mickey were facing in the same direction, at least one of them should notice.

It was Norman, of course, who saw me first.

"Hey, Danny!" he called from across the wading pool, where he was attacking Gus's short fat legs underwater and making him squeal. "Your brother wants you."

Mickey watched as Danny got up and came over.

"What's up?" Danny asked.

"Maintenance is going to Paul's to check electrical outlets, and Paul's got Bonkers in that pillowcase," I said.

"When are they coming?" asked Danny.

"That's just it! It could be any minute, it could be after dinner, it could be seven o'clock tomorrow morning. They didn't say," I told him.

Danny went over to the deck chair, where he'd left his shoes and towel, and followed me out the pool gate. Paul and I waited while he put on his shoes and then went around behind the community center to figure out what to do.

There stood Mickey, Gus resting on one hip.

"Okay," she said. "What's going on?"

"It's Bonkers," said Danny, pointing toward the pillowcase. "We've got to smuggle him around till it's safe for him to go home again." And he explained the problem.

Mickey's eyes shone. "Just like the Underground Railroad!" she said. "We have to get him to a safe house!"

"The Rats' Railroad," said Danny.

I nudged Paul just then, because something blue was

sticking out from around the corner of the building like the head of a snake and I realized it was the end of a snorkel tube. Norm the Nerd was using the snorkel like an ear phone to listen in.

"Norman!" yelled Mickey.

Norman came around the corner of the building. "Who's Bonkers?" he asked.

It was hopeless. We knew right then that if we didn't tell him, he'd spy and tease and whine until he found out everything he wanted to know.

"Norman," said Paul, "if you want to live, you won't tell *any*one about this. You got it?"

"Who's Bonkers?" Norman said again.

"He's Paul's cat," said Mickey, "and if you breathe one word to anyone about it, you'll be really, really sorry."

"Dead meat," said Danny.

"Roadkill," I added.

Norman sure doesn't scare easy. "We're not supposed to have cats," he said.

"Bonkers isn't just *a* cat, he's Cat of the Year!" said Danny. "A hero!" And he told Norman how Paul had to give him away but the cat came back again.

"If Miss Quinn finds out . . ." began Norman.

"If Quinn finds out from *you*, you'd better start running, Norman, because we'll get you. I mean it!" said Paul, looking as anxious as he was angry.

Norman looked around the circle as though he didn't believe us. It was about then I realized that we were treating Norman like the enemy. As long as he felt like an outsider, he wasn't going to cooperate with anyone.

"Listen, Norman," I said. "We really need you. You've got to help us."

"Well, *sure!*" Norman said. "Why didn't you just ask?"

Man, sometimes things are simpler than you think.

"Danny, if you and T.R. can keep him till nine this evening, we'll take him after that," said Mickey. "Bring him over then and I'll climb out on the roof of the toolshed and take him up to my room."

So Paul handed the pillowcase to me, and Danny and I headed home.

I wondered what Mom *would* say if she knew we were keeping Paul's cat. She'd certainly feel sorry for a cat that had walked fifteen miles to get back home, but maybe she and Dad thought alike when it came to rules. Maybe she'd say she was sure Paul could find someone who would give Bonkers a loving home. She really wants to make a go of it at Rosemary Acres, I know that, and wouldn't want to make waves.

"Here's what we do," said Danny. "I'll go in first and motion to you which door you should come in."

The problem was that Bonkers was going a little nuts in that pillowcase. Paul said they used to take him to the vet that way, but I had it slung over my shoulder, and Bonkers was starting to scratch and hiss.

I cradled the pillowcase in my arms, being careful to keep the open end closed.

"Easy, Bonkers," I said, trying to stroke his back through the cloth. "Easy, boy."

Danny was up at his window motioning me to the

front door. I went in quickly. I could hear pans rattling in the kitchen, and knew Mom was making dinner.

We got the cat up to my room, and Danny went down for a saucer, a glass of milk, and a piece of lunch meat.

"We're about to eat, Danny. Don't ruin your dinner," Mom called after him.

We poured milk in the saucer and tore the lunch meat into little pieces. Bonkers snapped at each piece as though it were about to get away, then chewed with his mouth open, making loud smacking sounds. When he was through, he sat licking his jowls, and then his paws, eyes half closed. Watching the cat grow sleepy reminded me of what had happened that afternoon at the pool.

"Guess what, Danny," I said. "Miss Clark knows."

"About the cat?" he asked, and then his eyes grew wide. "About her *underwear*?"

I nodded. "She cornered me at the pool. I told her everything."

Danny just kept staring at me, his mouth open.

"You know what she said?"

"The Juvenile Home?"

I shook my head. "She's going to ask us to house-sit some other time, but if we goof up again, she tells Mom everything."

Danny couldn't believe it. "She's not only a sexy babe, she's a *nice* sexy babe," he said.

Paul called. "I forgot to tell you about a litter box," he said. "Get an old cardboard box, put about three whole newspapers on the bottom so it won't leak through, and then tear another newspaper into strips and dump those in the box."

I went down to the basement. We had plenty of left-over boxes from our move, so I chose a wide shallow box, and followed Paul's directions. Bonkers seemed to think it would do.

"Dinner!" Mom called.

"Okay," Danny yelled back. We closed the door and went downstairs.

As we sat down at the table Danny said, "I think there's a catbird building a nest in the tree outside T.R.'s window, Mom. You heard it?"

"I doubt it," said Mom, putting some corn on the table along with some sliced tomatoes and pork chops. "Cat-birds build their nests in heavy shrubs and thickets."

We *would* have to have a teacher for a mom.

"Well, maybe it's got a nest down near Lake Tarragon, but comes up here and sings in T.R.'s tree," said Danny.

"I suppose it's possible," said Mom. "I haven't heard a catbird for years. Did you know they're related to the mockingbird? Sometimes they sing for hours on a warm night."

Bingo! I almost wished Bonkers would meow so Danny could say, "There! Did you hear it?" but except for a soft thump from upstairs, which Mom didn't seem to notice, all was quiet. Maybe this would be easier than we thought.

"Teachers have to be back in school next Monday, you know," Mom was saying, "so you guys are going to be on your own for two weeks. Think you can handle that?"

"Sure!" said Danny.

"Because if you can't, or if I *feel* that you can't, Aunt Mavis has said she'd come and be here during the day till you guys start school."

Oh, man!

"We can *handle* it, Mom!" said Danny. "I don't want Mave here."

"*Most* of the time, I trust you," said Mom. "But there are other times I'm not so sure. And the problem with trust is that once it's broken, it takes a long time to heal. I want you to remember that."

"You can *trust* us!" I said, knowing, at that very moment, there was a smuggled cat up in my bedroom.

The Answer Guy

It was Danny's turn to do the dishes, so I went right upstairs to see how Bonkers was doing. He'd found an old pen cap and was batting it around my floor, then chasing after it. I was sure Mom could hear that from downstairs, but I hoped she'd think it was me, playing around.

Grandma Flora called to ask how our visit went with Dad.

"It went okay," I told her from the hall phone as Danny took over the cat-sitting.

"Just okay? For two years, almost, you don' see each other, and the visit is only okay?"

"We had fun in the Badlands," I said.

"Don' lie to me now. You make up with your father? He going to come see you?"

"We said we'd get together more," I told her. "But he didn't say anything about moving back."

"*Ahhh,*" she sighed. I think Grandma Flora was hoping

the same thing we were, that Dad wanted to come back and that Mom would let him.

"Well, T.R., good or bad, he's still your father."

"I know."

"For better or worse, he's the only father you got."

"Yeah."

"And you got this grandma down in Florida who loves every hair on your head, don' you forget it. You tell Danny, too."

"I will," I said.

"Grandma loves every hair on your head," I told Danny.

Bonkers used the litter box once to pee, and I don't think there's any smell in the world worse than cat pee. I was glad I didn't have to keep him in my room all night.

At nine o'clock, Mom was putting a load of clothes in the washer in the basement, so I put the pillowcase over Bonkers again and slipped down the stairs to the front door with Danny.

"We're going over to Mickey's, Mom," Danny called down the basement stairs.

"I want you guys home by ten sharp," she called back.

Bonkers was getting tired of pillowcases. He'd scratched me when I tried to get it over him, but Mickey would be waiting, I knew.

Just as we'd planned, she was out on the roof of their shed, edging her way down the shingles on her bottom. The light in her room was out, so we could hardly see her in the dark, but Danny whispered, "Mickey?" and she said, "Yeah—over here."

"Where's Norman?" I asked.

"Up in the hallway; he'll let us know if anyone comes upstairs."

We stumbled over some lawn chairs, trying to maneuver our way to the shed, but just then the back door opened and Mickey's stepdad came out.

"O'migosh!" breathed Mickey.

Here's the difference between Danny and me—my first thought was to hide in the toolshed. But Danny just said, "Hi, Mr. Harris." And then we both remembered that his name isn't Harris because he's not Mickey's real dad, even though she calls him that.

"It's Freeman," whispered Mickey, and then, "Hi, Dad. Isn't it a great night?"

The short man stopped and looked around. He couldn't see very well in the dark either.

"Hello, Mr. Freeman," said Danny.

"What's going on?" the stepdad asked, more curious, it seemed, than angry.

"The Scarlino brothers," said Mickey. "We're just talking. It seemed like a great night to sit out on the roof."

Her stepfather grunted. "Well, I don't know about that. It's supposed to rain. I came out to fold up the lawn chairs and put them in the shed."

"Oh, sure," said Danny. "Need some help?" He handed the pillowcase to me and started folding up chairs, and I moved to the back of the yard, stroking

Bonkers through the cloth. Mr. Freeman was trying to see our faces, we could tell.

"Mickey," her stepdad said, "why don't you ask your friends in? You don't have to entertain them out here, you know."

"Oh . . . we were just talking. We've got to get home," said Danny.

"Yeah, I'm gonna go to bed soon," Mickey said. "Good night, guys. See you tomorrow."

In the second window, though, we could see Norman motioning us to stick around. We waited till Mr. Freeman went inside, then we made our way over to Norman's window.

He was leaning out, lowering a bucket on a rope.

"You sure of this?" Danny whispered to him.

"It's the only way," he whispered back.

"You'll have to start pulling as soon as we put the cat in, or he'll jump out," I told Norman.

"I'm ready," he said.

As soon as Danny had hold of the bucket, I wrapped the pillowcase tightly around Bonkers and set him in.

"Pull!" whispered Danny.

The bucket began to go up.

"*Meow!*" came a pitiful wail from inside.

"Norman!" yelled a voice from somewhere in the house. "I want you to pick up your bathing trunks and towel. You left them here in the hall again with your snorkel, and they're still wet."

The bucket came rapidly down again.

"*Meow!*" wailed Bonkers again.

"Okay, I'm coming, Mom," Norman yelled, as Mickey took his place at the window.

We held the pillowcase down until Mickey pulled on the bucket.

"Mickey, your suit's here, too!" came their mother's voice. "Honestly, if you kids can't remember to hang up your things . . ." The voice was getting louder. "What are you *doing* up here, anyway?"

The bucket came down at the speed of light, and Danny caught it just in time. Bonkers had one paw over the edge. The rope came down on me.

"Nothing!" said Mickey, her back to the window.

Her mother came to the window and peered out as Danny and I flattened ourselves against the side of the house.

"Well, keep this window closed. We've got the air-conditioning on," she said. And then the light went out.

"Now what do we do?" I asked Danny when we took off down the alley for home. "If we have to keep Bonkers overnight, he's going to stay in your room."

"Randall hasn't had a turn yet; maybe he'll take him," said Danny.

He stayed outside while I went upstairs and called Randall from our hall phone.

"Hey, man, why are you making such a big deal? Just lock the cat in a closet when maintenance comes, no sweat."

"He'd *meow*, Randall! All it would take is one loud yowl, and maintenance would report it to Quinn."

"Look," said Randall, the Answer Man. "Is Paul going to be home tomorrow?"

"Yes."

"The men are going to knock before they come in?"

"Sure."

"So here's what Paul does. Soon as the men knock, Paul locks the cat in his closet, turns on his radio full volume, and Bonkers can carry on all he wants. The men won't hear a thing."

I felt really stupid. I went down and told Danny what Randall said. Danny said he felt stupid, too. We returned the cat and the pillowcase to the Bremmers' and told Paul what to do when maintenance showed up the next day. The thing is, when maintenance *did* get to Paul's, they didn't check every room, only the electrical panel in the basement. But I don't know what we'd do without Randall.

Search Party

Okay, we solved this one, but once September came, then what? What if Mr. Bremmer was away, Paul was in school, and maintenance had to get into their house? What if Bonkers went bananas when everyone was gone and meowed so long and loud that the people on either side of the Bremmers heard? I kept telling myself that this was Paul's problem, not ours, but it wasn't true. The Desert Rats were in this together, and we liked Paul the way he was now. We didn't want him angry and moody anymore. We liked seeing his dad smile.

What happened next was on Monday. Mom had left for the school where she'll be teaching, and Danny and I were lazing about the house, trying not to think about the end of summer.

Then the doorbell rang, it was Paul, and for the first time since we'd met back in June, he didn't have either the scowl he'd had when he shot baskets or the happy look he got after Bonkers came back. Instead, he looked sad and scared—something we'd never seen on his face before.

"*What?*" I said. Danny got up from the couch and came to the door as Paul stepped inside.

"Bonkers is missing," said Paul.

"What do you mean, missing? Somebody took him?" Danny asked.

"No. I think we left the door open this morning when we were carrying groceries in, and he must have taken off. Dad's already left for a meeting in Chicago."

I let out my breath.

Randall rode up just then with his towel draped around his neck and balanced with one foot touching the bottom step. "Anybody want to go swimming?" he asked. And then he looked at me and said, "What's happening, Tree Roots?"

"Come on in," I said.

Randall got off his bike and came up the steps.

"Bonkers got out," I said, closing the door behind him.

"Trou-ble!" said Randall.

"Maybe he's heading back to that family in Aurora," I told Paul.

Danny nudged my arm, and I realized that was about the last thing Paul wanted to hear.

"I just don't understand it," Paul said. "Bonkers always hung around the steps before when we'd let him out back in Oregon. He never wandered away like this."

"Maybe he got a taste of the big outdoors and likes it," said Randall.

"That's what I'm afraid of." Paul sat down on our sofa

and put his head in his hands. It was as though we were seeing the real Paul for the first time—a guy who was hurting.

"Well, we got work to do," said Randall, taking the towel from around his neck and dropping it on a chair. "Better call the other Rats."

"I'll call Mickey," said Danny. He went to the phone and dialed her number. I guess when somebody *tells* you to call a girl, it's not so embarrassing. In about three minutes, the Desert Rats were sitting around our living room, Norman included.

Paul described his cat for Norman, who hadn't seen it yet. I don't know how I'll talk when I fall in love, but you'd think Paul was in love with his cat the way he talked about him.

"He's got yellow fur and the greenest eyes you ever saw. If you find him in the dark, in fact, all you can see are his eyes. If he likes you, he's got this really loud purr, and his tail—well, it's not as thick as a Persian's, but it's pretty thick."

"Hey," said Mickey, "if you find a yellow cat at all around here, it'll probably be Bonkers."

"What do we do if we find him?" asked Norman.

"Put him in a pillowcase," Paul said.

I went upstairs and got pillowcases for everyone, and then we set out in different directions to look for Bonkers. Paul said it didn't matter whether we looked in the same places he had or not, because a cat can be sitting under a bush you've passed by ten times, and maybe the eleventh time he'll come out.

I tried to think like a cat might think. I was used to thinking like a dog. I've always felt I was sort of Danny's dog, actually—his faithful companion, always there to look out for him and keep him out of trouble.

But now I had to be Bonkers for a while. I decided that the cat wouldn't try to go back to the family in Aurora, not after he'd gone to all the trouble to come back here. I didn't think he would run away just because he couldn't see out of a window, either. I think Randall was right—Bonkers had just got a taste of the big outdoors on his long journey from Aurora back to Rosemary Acres, and when Mr. Bremmer left the door open, Bonkers wanted to go out and get another dose.

If the cat used to hang around the steps back in Oregon, like Paul said, maybe he was doing the same thing here—just somebody else's steps, that's all. The problem with Rosemary Acres is that while the front yards all run together, the backyards are fenced in right to the alleys.

If Bonkers could find something in every yard to leap up on—a trash can or something—he could jump from there to the top of a fence and go leap-frogging from one backyard to another. And at Rosemary Acres, you don't just unlatch your neighbor's gate and walk in looking for a cat, the way we could at Aunt Cis's back in Chicago. You especially don't go around asking people who can't own cats if they've seen yours.

I wanted so much to be the one who found Bonkers. I figured Paul and I would be friends for life if I did.

I met Danny at the end of the alley after I'd climbed up on about seven garbage cans and peered over people's fences.

"No luck?" I asked.

Danny shook his head.

"Maybe somebody already found him and took him in—is hiding him just like Paul was," I said.

"That's what I was thinking," said Danny.

We met Mickey and Randall coming from the direction of the playground, and Norman and Paul coming down the block. There was no cat in anyone's pillowcase.

"I've *got* to find him!" Paul said, sounding desperate. And then, "It's all I've got left of Mom's—that's alive, I mean."

This time Paul didn't seem embarrassed opening up in front of us. I guess the Rats were coming together in a lot of ways. Being honest about how we felt was one.

"You think we should check Lake Tarragon?" Danny asked finally. "Maybe he can smell the fish in it."

"I already looked," said Paul, "but I suppose we could try again."

Danny's Desert Rats—all six of us now—turned the corner and started up the road toward Lake Tarragon, our pillowcases hanging out of our jeans pockets. The Rosemary Acres office is at the top of the hill across from the path that leads down to the lake, and when we reached the place where we'd cross over, we suddenly turned to stone. For there, coming down the sidewalk from the office, was Miss Quinn, resident manager, Bonkers in her arms.

Randall Does It Again

I guess my first thought was that at least she didn't have her hands around the cat's neck. But she might be on her way down to Lake Tarragon to drown him.

"Looking for something?" Miss Quinn said stiffly. Seeing Paul, Bonkers tried to turn himself around in Miss Quinn's arms, but she held on.

The Desert Rats were speechless. We didn't know what to say. If we admitted the cat was Paul's, the Bremmers were in big trouble. If we didn't, what would happen to Bonkers?

It was Danny who spoke first. "I'll bet you don't know how famous that cat really is," he said to Quinn.

She studied Danny a moment. "*This* cat?" She held Bonkers out in front of her as though offering him up as a sacrifice or something, and in that instant Bonkers dug in his claws, Miss Quinn let go, and Bonkers made a flying leap onto Paul's chest.

"Well!" said Quinn, rubbing her arm. "At least I know who he belongs to."

"He *is* famous!" I said, wanting to help out. "Paul gave him away, but he came back all the way from Aurora."

Then Mickey got into the act. "Just imagine it, Miss Quinn!" she said dramatically. "This poor little kitty climbed over rocks and waded through streams and crossed highways. He was hungry and wet and cold and . . ."

"It's August," said Miss Quinn, "and the temperature hasn't gone below sixty."

"But think of the *love!*" Mickey went on. "How many other cats would go fifteen miles to find their masters? The devotion! The loyalty!" And Mickey doesn't even *like* cats!

"Three different people phoned the office this morning to report a cat wandering across their patios," said Miss Quinn. "And when I opened the door to get the mail, here he was. You know the rules, Paul, and if we say yes to one resident, we'd have to say yes to anyone else who wanted pets."

"Would that be so awful?" I asked timidly.

"The board of directors makes the rules, not me," Miss Quinn told us. She reached out then and scratched Bonkers gently behind the ears. "He is a beautiful cat, but you'll have to find a new home for him, Paul. I'm sorry." She turned and went back up the sidewalk to the office.

We stared at each other and then at Bonkers, who was purring loudly now and snuggling down in Paul's arms. I knew Paul would never give him up. He and his dad would leave Rosemary Acres before they let Bonkers go again. And now that I was getting to know Paul better, I didn't want him to leave. None of us did.

"Stupid!" Paul said to his cat. You could just tell, though, by the way he looked down at Bonkers, that he'd probably never loved anything in his life as much as he loved him—except his mom, maybe.

"You could give him to Mr. Hillman to keep on his farm, and then you could visit whenever you wanted," Norman suggested.

It wasn't a bad idea—better than anything we'd come up with yet, and Hillman would probably take him. So would Aunt Cis, I'll bet, if I asked her. The problem was that Paul and his dad needed that cat as much as Bonkers needed them. I guess when you've got something warm in your arms that used to belong to your mother, it's the next best thing to hugging her, but I didn't see how we could ever explain that to the board of directors.

We all walked glumly back to Paul's, two in front of him, one on either side, and one behind, so that no one else would see Bonkers and complain.

"If he just hadn't got out!" said Mickey.

"He's got the brain of a flea," said Danny.

The only person who hadn't said a word so far was Randall, but as soon as we got inside Paul's with the door closed behind us, Randall said, "There's got to be a way to keep that cat."

"How? Turn him into a canary or something? Birds are allowed," said Danny.

"Let me think about it," Randall told him.

We were pretty quiet at dinner. Mom told us about the teachers' meeting at school, and how she was going to fix up her classroom, but finally she looked at us and said, "Have you boys been to a funeral today or what?"

"Actually, yes," said Danny, and I realized we didn't have to keep it secret anymore. We told Mom about Bonkers, about his long journey back from Aurora, and how we'd seen Mr. Bremmer smile for practically the first time all summer.

Mom's a real softie. Mothers are supposed to be, I guess. Danny was only halfway through the story before I saw tears in her eyes. I'll bet we could have kept Bonkers right here in this house with Mom's blessing.

"Poor cat!" she said. "Fifteen miles! Oh, the dear little thing!"

I began to think that if Mom acted this way when she heard the story, and if Mickey, who doesn't even like cats, would do what she could to save Bonkers, maybe we could just go around the whole development, door to door, with a petition to save the cat. A special exception to a rule, like Dad said.

We told Mom how Paul had orders to find another home for Bonkers, and how he just didn't feel he could give the cat up.

"If I get any bright ideas, I'll let you know," Mom told us. But the next day we could tell that the cat was the last thing on her mind; she was just too busy getting ready for school.

Two letters came in the mail, one from Mom's dad, Grandpa Gil, in Milwaukee, saying that he was coming for a short visit, and the next day we found the other one in our mailbox when we got back from Hillman's.

The Desert Rats had ridden over to the family cemetery plot near the back of Hillman's property, where a mulberry tree leaves streaks of red and purple on the tombstones below, like something out of a Stephen King novel.

But it's shady and cool in the little cemetery, and that's why we go there—it's the one place near Rosemary Acres, besides the woods down by Lake Tarragon, where you can count on it being cool. So we just hang out there and talk and see who can tell the wildest story, and when we get bored or thirsty or Norman gets weird, we go home.

And that's when Danny and I found the letter from Dad in our mailbox, along with my copy of *Cricket* and a magazine on mountain biking that Uncle Keith had given Danny a subscription to at Christmas.

Danny and I took the letter to the kitchen and opened some pop, then sat down to read it. Danny read it first, then passed it over to me without saying anything:

Dear Danny and T.R.,

I hope you're enjoying the end of August. It's dry here in California, and there's always the threat of forest fire.

I realize that our trip to North Dakota together was somewhat precipitous, so we weren't able to prepare for it the way I would have preferred, and obviously we couldn't absorb all there was to see unless we'd had more time. Still, I'm glad we did it, and hope you have some good memories. I can't let one incident go without comment, though.

It seems to me that neither of you understood the significance of what we were observing in the Theodore Roosevelt National Forest, but I feel I did the best I could to explain how the Badlands evolved. I was especially disappointed, then, that you chose to use the last two exposures on my camera in a silly prank, after having been advised to select your subject carefully. I can only trust that as you get older we'll have more things in common that we can share.

I've gone through my photographs and selected those I think might be especially memorable. You may want to start a scrapbook of our trips together, so I'm having copies made to send to you—with the exception of the last two pictures, of course.

Love, Dad

Mom came in while I was reading the letter and put her car keys on the counter.

"Mom," I said, looking up, "I know that when people get older they lose their hair, but do some people lose their sense of humor, too?"

Mom noticed the letter from Dad in my hand. Then she smiled. "T.R., some people just never had all that much to begin with, and it's a shame."

I was sitting out on the steps eating some grapes when the lawyers next door came home. At least, I think they're lawyers. They both wear dark suits, and they've both got dark briefcases, and they never smile. Lawyers or undertakers, one or the other.

"Excuse me," I said.

That was my first mistake, I guess. Both of them acted as though that little piece of wall separating their entrance from ours was supposed to make them invisible.

"Beg your pardon?" said the man, while his wife searched for the key in her purse.

"I just want to ask a question," I told him.

"Yes?" He was hot and impatient to get indoors.

"If you knew there was this cat, see, that had walked fifteen miles over deserts and mountains and everything to get back to his owner, and the owner wasn't supposed to keep him because the development didn't allow pets . . ."

"Does this have anything to do with Rosemary Acres?" the man asked.

"Yes. My friend Paul had to give up his cat, but now it's come back and Miss Quinn says it can't stay."

"And she's absolutely right," said the woman. "The last thing I want to see is a cat digging up my flower bed."

She and her husband went inside and shut the door. Undertakers. They *had* to be undertakers.

Miss Clark came out of the house across the street to walk down to the mailboxes.

"Hi, T.R.," she called, and acted as though she'd forgotten all about the underwear problem. That gave me the courage to walk out to the street and ask how she might feel about Bonkers.

"If there was a cat in Rosemary Acres you didn't know about, would you get upset?" I asked.

She studied me carefully. "Don't tell me you hid a cat in my house, too!" She *hadn't* forgotten what we did with her underwear.

I told her about Bonkers.

"Well, here's the way I see it," she said. "I feel sorry for Paul and his dad and the cat, too, but there are a lot of people in Rosemary Acres who love animals. I've always wanted a Labrador myself. If Paul gets to keep a cat, then I should have a dog. Right? The board of directors said no pets, so no pets it's got to be."

I began to see the problem. So much for a petition!

Danny and I went over to Paul's the next morning and sat on the living-room floor playing with Bonkers. Paul took a piece of string and put it under the rug in front of the couch with just a few inches sticking out the other side. Then he'd give a little tug on his end of the string, and the cat went nuts.

He'd crouch down in the attack position, his pupils dilating, muscles quivering, and the next time Paul tugged at the string, Bonkers would pounce. He'd roll over and over, trying to catch the string in his paws. Paul was down on the floor playing like a little kid–I'd just never seen him like this before. Once, though, when Danny and I were playing with the cat and Paul was watching, I noticed that his eyes looked wet.

"How long do you have to find a home for Bonkers?" Danny asked finally.

"Miss Quinn called Dad last night and said if the cat wasn't gone in a week, they'd have to ask us to move."

Mickey came by a little later with Gus. She said she'd seen our bikes outside, so she'd parked the stroller by the steps.

"Mom took Norm to the dentist, and I'm Gus-sitting,"

she said. She set him on the floor and the baby looked at the cat and cooed. Bonkers came over to sniff Gus, smelling the same smell we did, I guess, and turned away. Mickey doesn't seem to mind much when Gus has stinky diapers. I guess if you love someone enough, you even forgive his diapers.

"I just wondered if you'd thought of a solution," she said. "If there's anything I can do, Paul . . ."

"All I know is to take him to Hillman's farm and ask if they want him. But he wouldn't be mine anymore. I'd hardly ever see him. He'd probably either keep coming back here or he'd wander off—might even get hit by a car."

It was just about then the doorbell rang, and Randall walked in, carrying a weird-looking box. He was the only one of us who was smiling.

"What have you got to grin about?" Paul asked him.

"Necessity is the mother of invention," he said, putting the box down on the coffee table.

"Huh?" I said.

"That means that when there's a real need for something, somebody usually invents it."

"So what did you invent?" I asked.

"Something to save Bonkers," Randall told us. "Maybe," he added.

"What?" we all asked together.

Bonkers suddenly did an about-face in the middle of the floor and came over to the coffee table. He stood on his hind legs and sniffed the box.

"Actually," said Randall, "I didn't exactly *invent* it. I just got the idea."

"*What?*" we all asked again.

Bonkers was up on the coffee table now, moving slowly around the box. Randall picked it up and, as we all crowded closer, lifted one corner of the lid just a crack so we could see inside.

"Mice," said Randall.

The Grandfather Clause

Mice?" I said. I didn't see how that would help the problem at all.

"I invented this trap, see, and put it out in Hillman's field," Randall explained. "There's cheese and peanut butter inside, and when mice go in, they slide down this steep aluminum slide that I've greased, and then they can't get out again."

"So?" said Paul.

"So every day, one of us puts a mouse in Miss Quinn's office."

"She'll trap them and throw them out," said Danny.

"But they'll keep coming!" Randall grinned. "And that's when we tell her she can keep Bonkers there at night. As soon as she takes Bonkers, the mouse deliveries stop."

"You're going to give my cat to Quinn?" Paul asked.

"On loan. Just at night, see, when the mice come out. You've got to try something, man!"

Randall was right about that. School was starting soon and time was running out. We agreed we'd take turns going to the office with a mouse in a pocket so Quinn wouldn't get suspicious about any one of us. Actually, when you open the door to the Rosemary Acres office, there's a hallway you enter first before you're in the room where Quinn's desk is, and we realized we didn't have to go all the way in at all. We only had to open the door a crack and slip a mouse inside. Randall said he'd go first, only he was going to put two in, to make sure Quinn saw at least one of them.

Mickey had to take Gus on home, but the rest of us were waiting at the corner when Randall came back, and decided that for the rest of the day, one of us should be riding past the office at all times to check what was going on.

Danny and I said we'd take the first hour. Paul would relieve us after that, and then Randall. So the other guys went home and Danny and I rode slowly up and down the block, turning in wide circles at the end of the road each time and starting back again.

I don't know what we expected Quinn to do. Run screaming from the office with her hands in the air? That's something Aunt Mavis would probably do, and Miss Quinn and Aunt Mave have a lot in common. Mom, though, would probably try to think of some humane way to get rid of the mice, and Aunt Cis would just let them be. That's my guess.

"What are we watching for?" I asked Danny after a while.

He must have been thinking the same thing. "I'm not sure," he said. "How do we know she won't just put out d-Con and forget about it?"

"What's d-Con?"

"Poison."

I never thought about that. Sacrificing a mouse every day to a mousetrap or the jaws of a cat was bad enough, but a long slow death by poison? The mouse hadn't asked to get in Quinn's office, after all.

"In fact," Danny went on, "all she'll do when she sees one of those mice is call maintenance and turn the job over to them. Shoot. Let's go home."

We were just plain lucky, because we had passed the entrance to the Rosemary Acres office for about the fifteenth time when we heard the door open and, looking back, saw Miss Quinn standing against the open door staring down at the step, as though she were commanding something to leave.

Danny made a slow U-turn in the middle of the street and I followed.

"Boys!"

She'd seen us now and motioned us over.

"Yeah?" said Danny, riding up.

"All the maintenance men are at lunch, and I've got a small problem," she said.

"What's that?" asked Danny.

"I just saw a mouse run across the floor of my office. I was hoping if I held the door open, it would come out, but I don't think that's going to work."

Miss Quinn kept staring at the floor, but we were staring at Miss Quinn. She sure didn't know much about mice.

"They won't come out as long as you're standing there," I said.

"*They?*" said Miss Quinn, and I was afraid I'd blown it. But Danny covered for me.

"Where there's one mouse, there're usually more," he said. "In fact, if you see one in the daytime, there are usually a *lot* more, because most mice don't come out till night. That's what I've heard, anyway."

A look of horror crossed Miss Quinn's face. She and Aunt Mave *were* a lot alike.

"Do you think you could ride up to the store for me and pick up a trap or something? Poison?"

"*Euuuu!*" I said. "Boy, either way, it's an awful death."

"Well, the mice should have thought of that before they got in my office," said Quinn.

I couldn't believe she'd said that.

"The problem," said Danny, getting off his bike and peering around the doorway, "is that once they get in, they keep coming. They learn to avoid the traps and poison."

"I don't understand this! We've never had a mouse problem before!"

"Probably because Rosemary Acres was just too new. When fall comes, though, mice leave the fields and nest in houses. And there sure are a lot of fields out here," Danny told her.

"They have that great big barn on Hillman's farm!" Miss Quinn protested. "They can make all the nests there they want."

"Tell that to the mice," I said, and smiled politely.

But Miss Quinn wasn't amused. "I can't stand the thought of mice running around the floor," she said, shuddering.

"Yeah. They get in desk drawers and have babies and everything," I told her.

"What am I going to *do*?" she said anxiously.

Did you ever see a solution just fall into your lap like that?

"Well," said Danny, "maybe you could borrow Paul's cat till he finds a home for it. Grandpa Gil used to say that mice will stay away from a house that has cats."

I bet Grandpa Gil never said any such thing, but I wasn't going to worry about that now.

"Really? Well, I surely would feel better with a cat around, that's certain," said Miss Quinn. "Just a temporary solution, of course. I'll have to check it out with the board of directors, but I suppose we could tell the other residents that we only borrowed it for a few days."

"Sure," I said.

"We could go ask Paul if you want," Danny told her. "Unless he's found a home for Bonkers by now."

"Bonkers?"

"The cat. He used to see mice and go bonkers. The name sort of stuck."

"*Please* go ask," said Miss Quinn.

We got on our bikes again and ambled on up the street, but as soon as we turned the corner, we hooted and tore up the street toward Paul's. He heard us coming and opened the door.

"It worked!" Danny whispered, as we ran up the steps. "Quinn wants to borrow Bonkers for a few days."

Paul's mouth dropped open.

"Just like that?" he asked.

"Just like that!" I told him.

Mr. Bremmer was home now and came to the door with a sandwich in his hand. Danny explained what had happened at the Rosemary Acres office, and how he hoped we'd talked Miss Quinn out of using either traps or poison.

"Better take a litter box with you," his dad said, as we got Bonkers ready to go.

We helped put some litter in a cardboard box and then, Paul holding Bonkers in his arms, Danny carrying the litter box, and I, carrying his water dish, walked back up the hill to Miss Quinn's office.

She was still standing outside when we got there, and looked relieved to see the cat. We all went inside and closed the door.

"I appreciate this, Paul, especially since you can't keep the cat yourself," she said.

"Well, Bonkers will think it's a treat," he told her.

"I don't know where it went," Miss Quinn said, looking around. "But I saw it go right across the floor from my wastebasket to the bookcase and disappear behind the drapes."

"Boy, it could be anywhere!" I said, looking around the office.

Miss Quinn wrapped her arms around her body.

Bonkers had already gotten a whiff of something,

because he moved slowly around the room, tail straight out behind him, belly low to the floor.

"What I don't like about mice is they just dart out at you," Miss Quinn said. "They're not like spiders. You always know where a spider is, but with mice . . ."

"Bonkers will take good care of you," said Paul.

We set the box of litter in the rest room and the water dish under the sink. We were just getting ready to leave when, *whoosh!* A yellow smudge streaked across the floor.

Pounce!

The next thing we knew, Bonkers had a mouse in his jaws and was walking proudly, tail held high, around the room–prancing, actually–and looking at Paul as if to say, Where would you like it, O Master?

Quinn sucked in her breath, one hand to her throat. "*That* was fast!" she said.

"One down!" I crowed. Danny poked me.

Paul reached down and got Bonkers to drop the mouse into his hand. It wasn't hurt much, and Paul took it outside, crossed the road, and put it in the field that led down to Lake Tarragon.

"Behave yourself now," he said to Bonkers when he came back, and Miss Quinn thanked us again.

I don't know when we ever felt better. We felt like celebrating, in fact, so we called Mickey and Randall when we got home, and they both came over, Norman tagging along as usual. Danny put a half gallon of vanilla ice cream on the table in a bowl and we mashed up a package of Oreo cookies in it and stirred until the ice cream turned gray. Then we had a feast.

"You did it, Randall!" I said. "You brain!"

"You got that right, Train Ride," he said, and we laughed.

Then Mickey said it: "The problem . . ."

She didn't finish. She didn't have to. We all knew what the problem was. After Miss Quinn decided she didn't need Bonkers anymore, Paul still had to give him away. Unless we kept sacrificing mice, of course, which none of us wanted to do, and anyway, one day somebody was bound to find out.

Just before dinner that evening, Grandpa Gil arrived from Milwaukee. Gilbert's his real name. Gilbert Fitzpatrick, but we call him Grandpa Gil. Actually, Aunt Mave, Mom's sister, had called about ten minutes before he got here, wanting to know if he'd arrived all right. I said no, Gramps hadn't come yet, but had she heard about this big infestation of rodents here at Rosemary Acres? She just hung up.

So while Mom was calling Mave to say that she could stop worrying, we carried Gramps's bags down to the family room, where he'd sleep on our sofa bed.

"Well now, how goes it, fellas?" he asked, giving us both a hug.

"Good and bad," I told him, and explained about Paul's cat. "I sort of think Miss Quinn would let him stay around if she knew what to tell the board of directors."

"Why, that's easy enough!" said Gramps. "Invoke the grandfather clause, that's all."

"The what?" asked Danny.

"All Miss Quinn has to do is tell the other residents

that Bonkers was here long before Rosemary Acres was ever built. He *was*, you know—on this planet, anyway—so an exception has to be made in his case. It's legal. Lawyers use it all the time. All she has to suggest is that Rosemary Acres bend the rules for their resident mouse-catcher, and that if anyone else has a mouse problem, they can borrow Bonkers for the night."

Mom came downstairs with extra hangers for Grandpa Gil. "Dad, don't you go hatching wild schemes while I'm gone tomorrow," she said. "Remember what happened the last time you were here—you got us all in trouble with those fireworks."

"Now Kath, you enjoyed it as much as anyone, and you know it." Gramps laughed, and Mom laughed with him. She gave him a hug.

"It's *so* good to have you here," she said. "I miss Mom, you know."

"So do I, sweetheart, but I look at you and think of her," he said.

I guess that's the way Paul feels about his cat and his mom.

We sat around the living room talking till Grandpa started nodding off, and then Danny and I got sheets and made up his bed for him.

The next morning the Desert Rats all walked to the Rosemary Acres office to take Bonkers his breakfast, and Miss Quinn said that when she walked in, she'd found that Bonkers had caught another mouse and placed it on her desk blotter.

I was afraid that would put an end to it right there.

But then she said, "You were right. Where there's one mouse, there're probably more. Who knows *how* many more."

I felt sorry for the mouse, but glad to hear what she said next:

"I was talking to maintenance, and they think I ought to put out d-Con, but I told them I feel more comfortable with a cat because d-Con only works if the mice decide to eat it. It just sits there waiting for the mice to come to it. The cat goes to the mice!"

"They got radar," said Randall.

"They surely have something," said Quinn. "I don't think the board of directors will object, because nobody wants mice here. The big question is what I tell the other residents."

"Just use the grandfather clause," I told her. "Tell them that Bonkers was here before Rosemary Acres was ever built—he was, too, on this planet, anyway. And that you're going to make an exception for the resident mouse-catcher. And tell them that if anyone has a mouse problem, they can borrow Bonkers."

"*Hmmm,*" said Miss Quinn. "Somehow I feel I'm being conned here, but that just might work." She smiled.

"And I'll bet that if there are any more mice around here, they're so scared they're hiding good," said Danny. "They won't come out till you go home and turn out the lights, that's for sure."

"I hope so," she said.

And then we waited for Paul to say his piece, and held our breath while he did: "If you want, I could sort of be the caretaker," he told her. "I could pick up Bonkers every morning and return him to your office at night. Then you wouldn't have to explain to everybody who came in during the day what he was doing here, but you'd have him in the office when he could do some good."

Miss Quinn smiled again, even wider. "Okay," she said. "It's a deal."

The procession made its way back to Paul's again, with Bonkers in Paul's arms. We kept slapping Randall on the back, and there were high fives all over the place. There would be no more mouse problem at the Rosemary Acres office because we let the mice go. Meanwhile, Bonkers would get the credit, Paul would get his cat, and that was about the best thing that happened to the Desert Rats the whole summer.